The Northeastern Series

in Criminal Behavior

Advisor in Criminal Justice
to Northeastern University Press

Gil Geis

Armed Robbers in Action

Stickups and Street Culture

RiCHaRD T. WRiGHT & SCoTT H. DeCKeR

foreword by Neal Shover

NORTHEASTERN
UNIVERSITY PRESS
BOSTON

NORTHEASTERN UNIVERSITY PRESS
Copyright 1997 by Richard T. Wright and Scott H. Decker

Library of Congress Cataloging-in-Publication Data

Wright, Richard, 1951–
    Armed robbers in action : stickups and street culture / Richard T. Wright, Scott H. Decker
      p.   cm. — (The Northeastern series in criminal behavior)
    Includes bibliographical references and index.
    ISBN 1–55553–324–8 (cloth : alk. paper). — ISBN 1–55553–323–X
(pbk. : alk. paper)
      1. Robbery — United States.   2. Thieves — United States. I. Decker, Scott H.
II. Title. III. Series.
HV6658.W75   1997
364.15'52'0973 — dc21   97–14230

Designed by Christopher Kuntze

Composed in Aldus by G&S Typesetters, Inc., in Austin, Texas.
Printed and bound by Thomson-Shore, Inc., in Dexter, Michigan.
The paper is Glatfelter Supple Opaque Recycled, an acid-free stock.

MANUFACTURED IN THE UNITED STATES OF AMERICA
01 00 99 98 97   5 4 3 2 1

To Nigel Walker and D. J. West

Contents

Foreword

David Matza once noted that American criminologists histor-
ically were "highly vague and short-winded about the phe-
nomena they presume[d] to explain." He meant that those
who profess expertise about crime had shown a remarkable
reluctance either to get close to or to describe in detail their
subject matter. Matza's comment, as it happened, preceded by
only a few years an outpouring of ethnographic research on
street offenders and their pursuits. A broad range of crimes
and criminals have been sketched by investigators, but armed
robbers, offenders who usually terrorize, frequently injure,
and occasionally kill their victims have received little attention. In this book, Richard Wright and Scott Decker give us
what is thus far the most comprehensive description and
interpretation of urban, predominantly African American,
street robbers, and their daily lives and crimes. For Wright, it
marks nearly fifteen years of attention to thieves that began
with Trevor Bennett in the path breaking *Burglars on Burglary* (1984). Wright and Decker, in their earlier investigation
of burglars (*Burglars on the Job*, 1994) and now in this examination of the activities of robbers, work from a sample of active offenders that gives their analysis the unmistakable feel
of the real thing.

Much of the growing volume of ethnographic research
on thieves and other street-level criminals was conducted on

offenders known to, referred by, or under the control of criminal justice managers. Many research subjects, in fact, were imprisoned when they were studied. The picture that emerges from this corpus of research is of anything but highly skilled and specialized career criminals. The criminal calculus of street offenders includes utilities overlooked in decision-making models and also employs a distinctive metric. There is longstanding concern, however, that this research may be biased and may have limited general application to street offenders. Thieves who manage to avoid ensnarement and the crimes they commit may be different from the crimes and careers of their less fortunate criminal peers. Against this backdrop, *Armed Robbers in Action* takes on considerable importance. The value of research conducted on captive samples inevitably will turn on how widely findings reported here diverge from what was learned in prison-based studies. Readers may consider whether the picture painted by Wright and Decker is cause for reassurance or for heightened concern about data quality and the integrity of findings from earlier studies.

The notion that criminals choose to commit crime has held the attention and constrained the projects of academics and policymakers for nearly twenty-five years. This approach understandably highlights the theoretical and crime-control significance of offenders' decision making. Wright and Decker provide a fascinating picture of decision making by their subjects, one that shows the gap between the offenders' actions and crime-as-choice theory. Street-level robbers typically make decisions in contexts of hedonism and desperation in which the likely consequences of their acts are neither weighed carefully nor taken seriously. When offenders describe their crimes, they employ a rhetoric of utilitarianism that contrasts markedly with the fanciful attributions of motives and meanings sometimes suggested by interpreters who lack the first-hand knowledge gained by Wright and Decker.

Anyone today who dared echo Matza's indictment of criminological scholarship for its shallow empirical base would be quickly dismissed as uninformed. And yet the growth of a

strong ethnographic research tradition in criminology, paradoxically, has been matched generally by widening experien-
tial distance between criminological subject matter and the
worlds and lives of analysts. Although the potential payoff
from comprehending crime through the eyes of offenders is
taken for granted, growing numbers of criminologists know
crime and criminals only as lines in electronic data files. This
is apparent, for example, in ad hoc conceptual models of criminal careers developed and promoted without regard for findings from ethnographic studies. The picture of armed robbers
and their pursuits sketched by Wright and Decker is an important corrective to interpretations of offending that are uninformed by grounded knowledge of crime.

The criminal career paradigm that took shape with the as-
cendance of crime-as-choice theory incorporated a measure
of criminal intensity. This individual-level offending rate,
symbolized by the construct "lambda," is measured using
data from offenders' self-reported offense history. It is clear,
however, that a great many men who commit burglary, robbery, and other street crimes have only the vaguest notion
of how many crimes they committed in the preceding, say,
two years. At some point—and it is a point that is reached
rather early in offenders' history of law breaking—they all
run together. Assumptions about and measures of criminal
intensity based on offenders' numeric recall seem of dubious
value. Here and elsewhere Wright and Decker contribute to a
better-informed picture of street criminals. Their use of free-
ranging armed robbers and the light their findings shed on
offenders make *Armed Robbers in Action* captivating reading. The authors' extremely rich and detailed understanding
of offenders' daily lives, routines, and decisions coupled with
their thoughtful observations on crime control merit the
attention of all who want to understand and limit the harm
caused by armed robbery.

Neal Shover
University of Tennessee

Acknowledgments

Authors, like armed robbers, do not contemplate and complete their projects in a sociocultural vacuum. Their work inevitably is influenced and shaped by those around them. It is our good fortune to be surrounded by bright and tolerant colleagues, each of whom possesses an uncanny ability to be critical without being cruel. Bruce Jacobs, Janet Lauritsen, and Rick Rosenfeld gave freely of their time thoughout the entire research process. We probably imposed on them too often, but our project is much the better for their collective wisdom.

Dietrich Smith, fieldworker extraordinaire, took on the daunting challenge of finding active armed robbers and convincing them to talk to us. It is a tribute to his skill and daring that we more than doubled our most optimistic initial estimate of the final sample size. Eric Baumer, Rosalee Copeland, and Theresa Bosslet stepped in as emergency interviewers whenever the flow of willing subjects threatened to exceed the project's capacity to absorb them. Laurie Mitchell transcribed all of the taped interviews with blinding speed and pinpoint accuracy. Although a child of the suburbs, her ear for urban street talk is unrivaled.

Michael Stein carried out much of the secondary qualitative data analysis for our project—a task that required him to read and reread hundreds of pages of interview transcripts.

This is difficult, painstaking work, and Michael did it with enthusiasm and good cheer. For helping us to dig ourselves out from under a mountain of data, we owe him a special debt of gratitude.

Perhaps the most challenging aspect of any field-based research project involves reducing what one has seen, heard, and felt "out there" to written form. Here too we were lucky to be able to fall back on the counsel of wise and patient friends. Linda Jeffery read the entire manuscript, making many helpful editorial suggestions along the way. Trevor Bennett, Gil Geis, Cheryl Maxson, and Neal Shover also read and commented on much of what we wrote; the book is 20 percent shorter and 80 percent clearer for their efforts. Others who provided us with helpful advice as the writing progressed include Bob Bursik, Dave Curry, Dick Hobbs, Kimberly Leonard, Cathy McNeal, Jody Miller, and Al Wagner.

Our project was funded jointly by the Harry Frank Guggenheim Foundation and the U.S. National Institute of Justice (Grant No. 94-IJ-CX-0030). We are required to state that the points of view or opinions expressed in this document are ours and do not necessarily reflect those of the funding agencies. That said, the project that gave rise to our views and opinions about armed robbery would not have been possible without their financial backing. It took guts to fund such a controversial piece of work and we would like to thank them for their unwavering support.

Armed Robbers in Action

Give it up, motherfucker!
Don't move or I'll blow your brains out!
This is just a robbery.
Don't make it a murder.

— Anonymous

1 Studying Active Armed Robbers

An elderly woman cradles a small bag of groceries in one arm while fumbling for her car keys. As she does so, a young man surprises her from behind, puts a .38-caliber revolver to the back of her head, and demands her purse. Before the old woman has time to comply, the assailant wallops her on the side of the head with his pistol; he wallops her hard because, in his words, "I want the bitch to know that I'm not fooling." Blood trickling from her ear, the woman falls to the ground. Without a second's hesitation, the attacker grabs her handbag and runs off.

This is the criminal offense of armed robbery, which in most jurisdictions is defined as the use of a weapon to take property by force or threat of force. According to the Federal Bureau of Investigation (1995), a robbery is committed somewhere in the United States every fifty-one seconds. Each year, nearly two-thirds of a million Americans are robbed, six out of ten of them by armed assailants. And the weapon they are most likely to be confronted with is a gun.

What makes a person put a gun next to the head of another human being and demand money? This book aims to answer that question by examining how active armed robbers interpret their circumstances and prospects in the situation of real stickups. How do they decide to commit armed robberies? What does it feel like to participate in an armed robbery?

Why do armed robbers target certain people? How do they convince these people to obey their commands? Such questions can profitably be directed to robbers themselves. To date, their views have received scant attention from criminologists.

A few researchers have attempted to tap into the armed robber's perspective by interviewing prisoners serving time for such offenses (Conklin 1972; Einstadter 1969; Feeney 1986; Tunnell 1992). The results of their studies, however, must be treated with caution. Much criminal behavior is a direct response to the pressures and temptations of life on the streets. Prisoners are insulated from these powerful forces—are no longer under their spell—and thus may respond quite differently from how they would in the outside world. What is more, it is clear that the accounts offered by incarcerated offenders often are distorted by the prison environment. No matter how much inmates are assured otherwise, many will continue to believe that what they say to researchers will get back to the authorities and influence their chances for early release. And even if this does not seem likely, why take the chance? Consequently, inmates are inclined to put the best possible spin on their previous criminal activities. Further, the experience of being apprehended and punished can alter how prisoners retroactively perceive the actions that brought about their downfall. By definition inmates are failed criminals. As Geis (1994:x) reminds us: "It is one thing to talk about failure, another to discuss contemporaneously behavior that is succeeding but which at any moment may end disastrously." Although a survey of incarcerated armed robbers found that only 27 percent of them believed that robbery was worth the risk (Figgie International 1988), presumably 100 percent of them felt it was worth the risk when they decided to commit the stickup that led to their capture.

Criminologists long have been aware of the limitations of research on prisoners. More than a quarter of a century ago, Polsky (1969:116) called for an end to such work in favor of field-based studies of active criminals, warning that "we can no longer afford the convenient fiction that in studying criminals in their natural habitat, we would discover nothing really important that could not be discovered from criminals behind bars." Nevertheless, most researchers remain unwilling to deal directly with offenders "in the wild." That reluctance is attributable to a variety of factors; everything from the inconvenience of inclement weather to the possibility of grave personal injury mitigates against dealing with serious criminals in a real-world setting. The most important reason for this reticence probably is the common belief that it is too difficult even to find a substantial number of active offenders, let alone convince them to cooperate in a social science research project.

Increasingly, this belief is being called into question. Recent research on active residential burglars, for example, has demonstrated that it is possible to locate offenders and secure their cooperation outside criminal justice channels (e.g., Cromwell et al. 1991; Rengert and Wasilchick 1989). Similarly, there have been numerous street-based studies of gang members (e.g., Decker and Van Winkle 1996; Hagedorn 1988; Moore 1991; Padilla 1992; Sanders 1994), many of whom were involved in serious delinquency.

There even has been one small-scale investigation into the decision making of active armed robbers. Through observation and interviewing, Merry (1981) explored how seven juvenile robbers operating in a public housing complex chose their victims and located spots for their stickups. Her study attracted considerable attention from crime prevention experts because it called into question the notion that criminals could be tricked by symbolic architectural changes into believing that an otherwise good robbery site was too risky for them (Murray 1983).

Merry's conclusions must be regarded as tentative because they come from a study of a few offenders who may not be typical. That all of the robbers were juveniles raises questions about the general applicability of her results. Moreover, she did not consider the total decision-making calculus of the robbers, but rather focused on matters related to the immediate physical surroundings of their crimes. This is a serious shortcoming; the impact of environmental factors on the decision making of offenders must be tempered by whatever mental state caused them to contemplate an offense in the first place.

There is a need for a larger and more broadly based investigation of the perceptual mechanisms underlying the decision making of active armed robbers. Such an investigation could shed new light on the ways in which motivational factors, situational characteristics, and environmental cues come together in the mind of the criminal so as to cause the offense to be committed. A full understanding of this process is crucial to the successful prevention of armed robbery (National Research Council 1993). It is only through knowing how armed robbers perceive the context of their crimes that we can hope to ameliorate the conditions that give rise to these offenses. As Bennett and Wright (1984:181) have observed, "Unless a crime prevention strategy is perceived by potential offenders as a constraint on crime, it is unlikely to have a preventive effect."

THE PRESENT STUDY

The idea of studying armed robbery through the eyes of those currently engaged in such crimes arose while we were conducting fieldwork with a group of active residential burglars on the streets of Saint Louis, Missouri (Wright and Decker 1994). In the course of that research, we encountered fourteen offenders who were committing armed robberies as well as breaking into dwellings. This convinced us that it might be possible to make contact with a larger number of active armed robbers and, from doing so, gain a more complete understanding of how they go about their business.

A field-based study of armed robbery seemed important to us because robbery, perhaps more than any other offense, fuels the fear of crime that undermines the quality of life for urban residents. As Conklin (1972:4) has put it, "Although the public certainly fears murder and rape, it is probably fear of robbery . . . which keeps people off the street, makes them avoid strangers, and leads them to lock their doors" (see also Wilson and Boland 1976). There are good reasons for city dwellers to be especially fearful of robbery. Robbery is a common feature of the urban landscape—far more common than murder or forcible rape—and poses a serious risk of injury or death. One in three robbery victims sustains at least minor injuries during the offense (Reaves 1993). More than 10 percent of all homicides occur in the context of a robbery (Cook 1991).

Beyond a pragmatic concern for personal safety, racial prejudice undoubtedly accounts for some of the fear that robbery engenders in the population. Unlike other forms of criminal violence, armed robbery often is an interracial event in which a white victim is confronted by a black offender. The offense can both provoke and reinforce racial stereotypes in which blacks are perceived to be predatory and violent. Hacker (1992:187) makes this point forcefully: "For white victims caught in interracial robberies the loss of cash or valuables is seldom their chief concern. Rather, the racial character of the encounter defines the experience." Robberies have done much to exacerbate racial tensions in America's cities.

Moreover, armed robbery bridges property and violent crimes. On its face, robbery appears to retain elements of planning and calculation associated with property offenses. Hence it may be preventable by well-designed deterrence and environmental change measures, strategies that require a firm grasp of how offenders think and act in real-life circumstances (e.g., Ekblom 1987; Feeney 1986).

Armed robbery is a serious problem in Saint Louis. In 1994, for example, the city had 6,025 stickups reported to the police and ranked second in the nation in robberies per 100,000 population (Federal Bureau of Investigation 1995). Such statistics, however, obscure the fact that armed robberies are not evenly distributed throughout Saint Louis. In general, robbery rates increase as one moves from the predominately white south to the predominately black north of the city, with the very highest rates in and around the most economically deprived black neighborhoods. Not only are these neighborhoods extremely poor, but they also have many related social problems, including high unemployment rates, large numbers of female-headed households, and widespread alcohol and drug abuse. Crack cocaine and heroin are sold openly, often by youths in their early teens, and attract a steady flow of customers. Physically, the areas resemble a war zone, with abandoned, burned-out, or boarded-up buildings punctuating each block, junked cars standing in litter-strewn vacant lots, and gang graffiti sprayed on almost every available wall. Groups of young to middle-aged men congregate on the street corner, insulting one another's sexual prowess, getting high, and looking for an opportunity to make some fast cash.

This is a man's world; there are very few female "regulars." Many women, though, are linked tangentially to such groups as wives and girlfriends. These women seldom associate with their men on the streets; their social groups are made up of their children, girlfriends, and mothers. The females most likely to be on the corner are prostitutes trying to earn money to sustain their drug habits.

It was on the desolate streets of these desperate neighborhoods that we located and subsequently interviewed eighty-six currently active armed robbers, focusing specifically on their thoughts and actions during the commission of their crimes. Our interviews were semistructured and conducted in an informal manner, allowing the offenders to speak freely. This approach created a more relaxed atmosphere and raised the confidence and level of cooperation of the robbers. Interviews usually lasted between one and two hours, with a great amount of time devoted to explaining questions and discussing answers. We believe that the offenders thought seriously about the questions put to them and responded truthfully. This is not to suggest that they never lied to protect themselves or embellished their accounts to impress us. Almost surely, some of them occasionally resorted to such tactics. Nevertheless, we do not believe that this happened often enough to undermine the overall validity of our findings.

The truthfulness of what the offenders told us could be monitored by questioning vague or inconsistent responses more directly. For those who agreed to take us to the scene of a recent stickup, we could check some of what they said during the interview through direct observation of the setting. Beyond this, sometimes we were able to compare descriptions of the same robbery incident offered by two or more co-offenders. Even though the co-offenders were interviewed separately, often weeks apart, their accounts generally corresponded closely. Initially we had hoped to check the arrest records of our robbers to determine the accuracy of their reports regarding previous contact with the criminal justice system, but this proved to be impossible. All but a few refused to provide their real name and date of birth; none was prepared to reveal his Social Security number.

Numerous opportunities arose during our research to verify that interviewees truly were armed robbers and that what they told us about their stickups was true. The most dramatic of these opportunities involved an offender who claimed that he was using a knife to commit his robberies because no one would lend him a gun. He said that knives were not good weapons for robbery and that he was increasingly fearful that someone would manage to overpower him and take his knife. He was killed that night when an intended robbery victim grabbed his weapon and stabbed him in the chest.

Another person we interviewed showed us a hand peppered with fresh pellet wounds—injuries sustained the day before when a robbery victim fired a shotgun at him as he fled the scene. Several other offenders displayed healed bullet wounds to us, which they said resulted from botched robberies. One respondent was interviewed while on the run from the police; he had mistakenly been released from the Saint Louis City Workhouse, where he was serving time for a parole violation after an armed robbery conviction. A number of interviewees were arrested on robbery charges sometime after we had spoken to them. Taken together, such incidents convinced us that we were dealing with serious armed robbers.

We asked the offenders to tell us as much as they could about their "typical" approach to committing armed robberies, concentrating as far as possible on their most recent offense. Throughout their recitals, we prompted them with questions regarding such things as motivation, victim selection, securing compliance, and escaping from the scene. We were careful to insure that, for each of these component parts, the offenders were describing a situation that was typical for them. Our aim was to get a thorough overview of the way in which they normally carried out their armed robberies.

Additionally, we took ten of the robbers to the site of a recent holdup for which they had not been apprehended and asked them to reconstruct the crime. Visiting crime scenes with the offenders allowed us to explore more fully with them how situational and spatial features of the setting contributed to the offenses. Here, too, we questioned the robbers closely about the extent to which various elements of the crimes described were typical. Thus we were able to develop a picture of the ways in which the offenders in our sample typically went about committing armed robberies. It is that information that makes up the bulk of this book.

CHARACTERISTICS OF THE SAMPLE

The demographic characteristics of our sample are presented in table 1. As can be seen, all but three of the offenders were black. In this respect, the sample does not reflect the racial

TABLE 1: Demographic Characteristics of the Sample

	Number of Offenders	Percentage*
RACE		
Black	83	97
White	3	4
Total	86	101
SEX		
Male	72	84
Female	14	16
Total	86	100
AGE		
Under 18	14	16
18–29	35	41
30–39	22	26
40 and over	15	17
Total	86	100

*Percentages do not total 100% owing to rounding.

composition of the population of arrested robbery suspects for the city of Saint Louis in 1993, the year immediately preceding our research. The Saint Louis Metropolitan Police Department's *Annual Report* (1994) indicates that 18 percent of robbery arrestees in that year were white and 82 percent were black. No doubt the racial composition of our sample is a reflection of the social chasm that exists between blacks and whites in the Saint Louis underworld. Black and white offenders display a marked tendency to "stick to their own kind" and seldom are members of the same criminal networks. Successfully making contact with active black armed robbers proved to be of almost no help to us in locating white offenders. All three of the white armed robbers included in our project were recruited through one particular network of black street criminals; two of them—both female—were linked to this network through their black boyfriends, while the third had become a member through his addiction to "crack" cocaine.

The sex distribution of our sample also differs somewhat from the population of arrested robbery suspects in Saint Louis. Fourteen of the offenders we interviewed (16 percent) were female, compared to only 7 percent of the robbery arrestees in the city in 1993. This is not surprising; given the statistical rarity of female robbers, we had made a special effort to recruit enough of them to enable us to explore potential differences between their perspective and that of their male counterparts. Although recent research has concluded that males and females generally approach their offenses in similar fashion (see, e.g., Decker et al. 1993; Sommers and Baskin 1993), it remains unclear whether such a conclusion is warranted for men and women actively involved in serious criminal violence. Common sense suggests that violent crime is where possible differences between male and female offenders should be most pronounced.

A substantial number of juveniles—fourteen (16 percent of the total)—were located for the project. The inclusion of such offenders broadens the research meaningfully because an increasing proportion of arrested robbers are under eighteen years of age (Federal Bureau of Investigation 1995), and this has fueled a national debate about the factors underlying youthful violence. Juvenile offenders, however, are omitted in robbery studies based on prisoners because access to them is legally restricted and they usually are detained in facilities separate from adult criminals. As a result, little currently is known about how juvenile armed robbers perceive the social and physical environment of their stickups (but see Merry 1981).

We asked the robbers to estimate the total number of stickups in which they had participated. To improve the accuracy of their recall, we posed three orienting questions: (1) How old were you when you committed your first armed robbery? (2) Have you experienced any significant gaps (e.g., periods of incarceration) in your criminal career? and (3) Has your level of offending fluctuated over time? The subjects typically first offered a very rough estimate of how many armed robberies they had carried out. Then they were prompted with additional questions about variations in their rate of offending over the course of their lives. Even so, most of them found it impossible to specify the exact number of offenses they had committed. One put it this way: "I don't know how many robberies I done, but it's a lot because I'm twenty and I started doing 'em when I was about fifteen or sixteen. I would say I done at least more than fifty." In the end, we recorded what the offenders agreed was a conservative estimate of the number of lifetime armed robberies, believing that this strategy would yield a reasonably trustworthy measure of minimal robbery involvement, albeit at the cost of underrepresenting the criminal experience of many in our sample. The responses to this question are summarized in table 2.

Better than two-thirds of the sample (71 percent) admitted to ten or more lifetime armed robberies. (In cases where subjects estimated their total number of stickups in terms of a range, such as five to ten, we used the lower figure in our calculations.) Included in this group are thirty-one offenders who had committed at least fifty armed robberies. At the other extreme are twenty-five individuals who said they had participated in nine or fewer armed robberies. Thus our sample consists predominately of experienced armed robbers, but it also includes a substantial proportion of relative novices.

The measure of lifetime armed robberies, of course, does not provide an estimate of the rate of offending. For that, one would have to calculate "lambda" (Blumstein and Cohen 1979)—that is, the average number of stickups per year—for each offender. In theory, calculating lambda is a simple matter

Table 2: Number of Lifetime Armed Robberies

	Number of Offenders	Percentage
Fewer than 10	25	29
Between 10 and 49	30	35
More than 49	31	36
Total	86	100

of dividing the total number of armed robberies committed by the total number of years at risk. In practice, however, this is extremely difficult. The difficulty inheres in the inability of offenders to provide even modestly precise estimates for either the numerator or denominator. As noted, most of the armed robbers we interviewed had only a vague notion of how many crimes they had carried out over the course of their careers. Similarly, few could recall accurately such things as the age at which they committed their first crime or the total amount of time they had spent "off the street" (and hence not at risk for lawbreaking) in jail or prison. Lambda estimates, therefore, are bound to be highly inexact, if not downright misleading. Recognizing that, we decided against using this measure. Suffice it to say that, when we interviewed them, many of our subjects were offending at a high rate: eighteen (21 percent) said they currently were doing more than one armed robbery a week. Other subjects had gone for a substantial period of time without committing any stickups at all.

Table 3 sets out whether, and to what extent, those in our sample have come into contact with the criminal justice system. Three of the offenders, it can be seen, had never been arrested for any serious offense. Obviously, such offenders would have been excluded had we based our study on a jail or prison population.

Perhaps a more relevant measure, however, is the experience of the offenders with the criminal justice system on charges of robbery. Most previous studies of the robber's perspective not only have been based on incarcerated criminals but also have used the charge of robbery as the basis for subject selection (e.g., Einstadter 1969; Figgie International 1988; Tunnell 1992). Of the eighty-six offenders in our sample, twenty-eight (33 percent) had no arrests for robbery, and twenty-three (26 percent) had one or more arrests, but no convictions for the offense. Put another way, roughly six out of every ten offenders we interviewed would not have been included in a study of incarcerated robbers. This inoculates

Table 3: Contact with the Criminal Justice System

	Number of Offenders	Percentage*
Ever arrested	83	97
No arrests	3	4
Total	86	101
No armed robbery arrests	28	33
Arrested for armed robbery, no convictions	23	26
Convicted of armed robbery	35	41
Total	86	100

*Percentages do not total 100% owing to rounding.

our research against the charge that it reflects only the views of "unsuccessful" offenders.

From a crime prevention standpoint, armed robbery presents a daunting challenge because the targets of such offenses are so diverse, including both individuals and commercial establishments. Understanding the cues that offenders use to select victims on the street may be of little help in devising ways to make business premises less attractive targets. Accordingly, we wanted to be sure to interview not only offenders who had committed street robberies but also those who had robbed commercial establishments. Table 4 indicates the usual armed robbery "style"—street or commercial—adopted by members of our sample. As the table shows, most of the offenders—seventy-three (85 percent)—usually committed their armed robberies on the street. By contrast, ten of them (12 percent) showed a marked preference for commercial offenses. Three of those we interviewed claimed to have no dominant robbery style, having committed street and commercial holdups in roughly equal proportions. This puts us in

TABLE 4: Typical Armed Robbery Style

	Number of Offenders	Percentage
Street robbery	73	85
Commercial robbery (e.g., confectionery shops, jewelry stores)	10	12
50/50	3	3
Total	86	100

a good position to be able to explore the decision-making strategies employed by armed robbers across a variety of target types.

Table 5 summarizes the previous criminal experiences of those in our sample over both the long and the short term. During the course of our interviews, we asked the offenders whether they had ever committed other types of crimes besides armed robbery. Almost all of them who answered the question—eighty-two of eighty-five (96 percent)—admitted that they had. The offenses most often reported were theft, burglary, assault, and drug selling.

We also asked the offenders whether they had committed offenses other than armed robbery during the month prior to being interviewed. Roughly two-thirds of them—fifty-three of eighty-six (62 percent)—claimed to have done so; almost a third said they had sold drugs, and a quarter reported committing various sorts of theft. Thus, while it may be convenient to think of these subjects as "armed robbers" for the purposes of the present study, it is important to remember that the majority of them are more criminally versatile than such a label implies. That said, most of the offenders were quite happy to be called armed robbers (or, in their words, "stick candy men"), suggesting that this designation carries some status in the social circles in which they travel.

In short, our sample was overwhelmingly black and poor, its members having been recruited on the streets of some of the most seriously deprived inner-city neighborhoods in

TABLE 5: Nonrobbery Offenses Committed

	In Lifetime		In Previous Month	
	Number	Percentage	Number	Percentage
Theft	53	62	22	26
Auto theft	22	26	6	7
Drug sales	50	58	26	30
Burglary	53	62	6	7
Assault	47	55	12	14
Prostitution / pimping	2	2	1	1
Forgery/fraud	10	12	1	1
Murder	8	9	0	0
Kidnapping	1	1	1	1
Public order crimes (e.g., interfering with arresting officer)	3	4	1	1
Other property crimes (e.g., receiving stolen property)	2	2	0	0

Saint Louis. Otherwise, the sample was quite ecumenical, comprising offenders who were male and female, juvenile and adult, successful and unsuccessful, experienced and inexperienced, and high rate and low rate. This was crucial for our research, since we aimed to encompass the diversity of views found among the population of active armed robbers who live and ply their trade in the toughest areas of the city.

LOCATING THE OFFENDERS

We employed a "snowball" sampling procedure (see Sudman 1976) to locate active armed robbers. This procedure required us to use "chains of referrals"—making contact with offenders and asking them to introduce us to criminal associates, who in turn were asked to refer others (see Watters and Biernacki 1989). This strategy may appear easy enough, but in practice it can be difficult to implement. The most obvious problem involves developing the initial contacts necessary to set each new referral chain into motion. How does one go about finding that first active armed robber?

In our burglary study, we had initiated referral chains by using a specially recruited fieldworker who was well known and respected by several groups of black street criminals operating in and around Saint Louis. This person, an ex-offender who had retired from crime after being shot and paralyzed in a gangland-style execution attempt, earlier had supported himself for many years as a highly skilled thief. He had been arrested just a few times and never been convicted. As a thief, he had acquired a solid reputation among his fellow criminals for both toughness and integrity. Trading on his reputation, our contact man relied mostly on tips provided by streetwise acquaintances to gain introductions to currently active residential burglars.

Through this street-based networking, the fieldworker widened his circle of criminal contacts. Because he scrupulously honored his promise to protect the confidentiality of those who took part in the burglary project, he retained his reputation for trustworthiness. Fortunately, we were able to call on his services again to help us find active armed robbers. Nevertheless, starting the referral process proved to be more difficult than we had anticipated. Our first idea was to reestablish contact with the fourteen offenders interviewed for the burglary study who also were committing armed robberies. But two of them had died, two were imprisoned, and the rest had dropped out of sight.

Accordingly, the fieldworker had to fall back on his street connections to locate active armed robbers; he began by approaching former criminal associates. All were still active offenders, and he found three who currently were doing armed robberies. He explained the research to them, stressing that it was confidential and that the police were not involved. He also informed them that those who agreed to be interviewed would be paid fifty dollars. He then asked the contacts to put him in touch with offenders actively involved in committing armed robberies, saying that we would pay them ten dollars for each referral. Previous experience had convinced us that such payments, however small, were necessary if we hoped to receive a reasonable number of introductions to offenders. It is a cardinal rule of street life that one should never do anything for nothing.

Figure 1 outlines the networks through which the offenders were located. It also illustrates the pace at which these networks were expanded. Perhaps the best way to clarify the recruitment process is to select a subject, say, No. 56, who is situated about halfway down the figure just to the right of center, and identify the chain of referrals that led us to him. In this case, our fieldworker contacted a female acquaintance who made her living exclusively through nonviolent street crimes. She introduced us to three active armed robbers—Nos. 15, 16, and 21—but, more importantly, she also put us in touch with one of her male friends, another petty criminal, who helped us find more than two dozen subjects. Among these subjects was No. 24; he referred us to three additional offenders, including No. 36. Offender No. 36, in turn, provided us with two further contacts, one of whom—No. 50—introduced us to five more active armed robbers; the last of these robbers was No. 56. This procedure is similar to that described by Watters and Biernacki (1989) in that the majority of respondents were not referred directly by the research staff. Instead, respondents came to us through the efforts of various actors in the street scene, such as heroin addicts, gang members, and petty criminals. We almost certainly would not have been able to locate many of these individuals on our own, much less gain their cooperation.

Buried within figure 1 are various indicators of the difficulties we encountered in constructing our sample. Note, for instance, that Offender No. 04, the first person contacted by our fieldworker, referred three other robbers to us prior to being interviewed himself. When initially approached about the project, he denied any personal involvement in robbery,

Figure 1. Evolution of Snowball Sample by Week

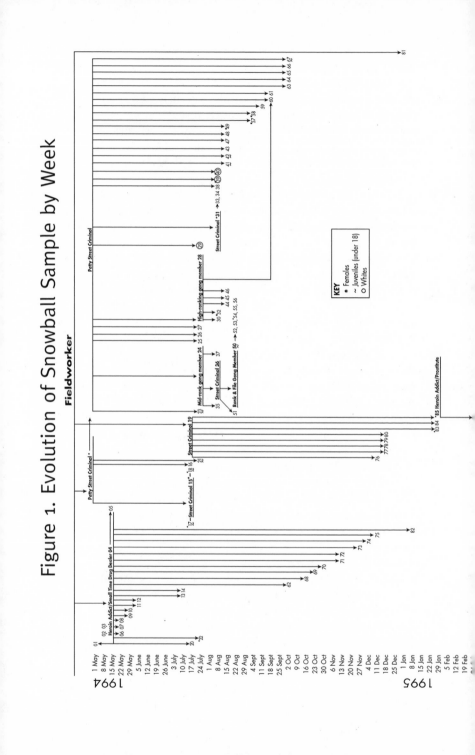

but assured us that as a junkie and street corner heroin dealer he came across many people who did commit such crimes. Only after being named as an accomplice by another offender did he admit to having taken part in the occasional stickup. He explained that he had not admitted his involvement earlier because he was worried about being set up for an arrest.

As can be seen, Offender No. 04 went on to provide us with many more referrals. Indeed, he stepped in as a backup fieldworker when, early in the project, our original fieldworker showed little interest in the job and went for over a month without recruiting additional interviewees. Desperate to keep the recruitment process on track, we turned to Offender No. 04, agreeing to pay him fifty dollars for each subject he referred to us. This worked well in expanding our network in the short term, but it generated considerable resentment on the part of the original fieldworker, who quickly regained his enthusiasm for the project. Thereafter, we were faced with the need to keep the two men apart; interviews had to be staggered accordingly, and this further complicated our attempts to build a suitable sample.

Given the tensions between our contact men, we had to be careful, lest we be perceived as playing favorites. Each brought his own unique mix of street connections to the project, and we did not want to alienate either one for fear of closing off our only conduit to potentially important subgroups of active robbers. The offender samples generated by the two men had different demographic characteristics. Almost all of the active armed robbers located by Offender No. 04 were older, black males, whereas our main fieldworker was able to recruit a more diverse range of offenders, including a sizable number of juveniles, over a dozen females, and several whites.

Interestingly, none of the subjects referred by Offender No. 04 seemed willing to put us in touch with fellow armed robbers directly; they insisted on using him as an intermediary. Our sense is that he kept a tight rein on the referral process, undoubtedly because he wanted the fifty dollar finder's fee. Nor did Offender No. 04 have any success in penetrating networks beyond the one in which he himself was a member. The project fieldworker, who admittedly has a personal ax to grind, claims that this lack of success is due to Offender No. 04's low street status and inability to inspire trust beyond his immediate circle of criminal acquaintants. There may be some truth in this claim. We know, for example, that Offender No. 04 has a history of robbing illicit crap games and street corner crack dealers; in doing so, he has made deadly enemies and thus needs to "watch his back" wherever he goes, especially when traveling outside the boundaries of his own neighborhood.

The most serious recruitment problem that arose during our fieldwork concerned Offender No. 81. He agreed to talk to us, despite his deep suspicion of our motives, only after being assured repeatedly by the project fieldworker that we were not working for the police. During our interview, it became clear that he was a well-connected armed robber and could serve as a valuable source of referrals. When asked if he would be willing to introduce us to his associates, he expressed some reluctance but, after considerable reassurance that we were trustworthy, finally consented. As figure 1 indicates, however, this never happened; he was arrested and charged with armed robbery within hours of speaking to us. We had no hand whatsoever in his apprehension. Nevertheless, several of our street contacts report that he continues to believe that we were responsible for his arrest.

Beyond these difficulties, we faced the predictable problems common to virtually all fieldwork involving hidden or deviant populations. Contacts that initially appeared to be promising turned sour and had to be dropped. Even productive contact chains had a tendency to dry up over time. One of our most challenging tasks involved determining whether potential subjects met the criteria for inclusion in our research. To be eligible, offenders had to be currently active armed robbers; that is, they had to have committed an armed robbery within the past month. The requirement seems straightforward but often was difficult to apply. The penalties for armed robbery are severe, and many of the offenders were evasive about the precise date of their last holdup. In such cases, we frequently had to rely on the fieldworker and other members of the sample to verify the eligibility of potential subjects. Some of those taking part in the project turned out to have last offended outside of our original one-month time limit. Because it seemed ill advised to turn away potentially valuable respondents to adhere to what was, after all, an arbitrary operational definition, subjects who clearly (1) saw themselves as being currently active and (2) were regarded as such by other offenders sometimes were included. Also, we did not want to exclude offenders who, because they planned their crimes in great detail and often netted large sums of cash as a result, went for long periods between offenses. Moreover, as already noted, we were anxious to ensure that our sample included a number of armed robbers who fell outside the statistical mainstream of such offenders (e.g., females), even if this sometimes meant bending our eligibility rules a bit.

The representativeness of a sample drawn from criminals at large in the community can never be determined conclusively because the parameters of the total population are unknown (Glassner and Carpenter 1985; Watters and Biernacki 1989). In recruiting our sample, we sought primarily to encompass, as far as possible, the diversity of perspectives on committing armed robberies found among a population of active offenders. To do so, we initiated the sampling process through four different street contacts in an attempt to reduce the chances of tapping into just one criminal network of like-minded offenders. Further, we questioned subjects about how their views might differ from those of other offenders in their social circle. The few times differences were reported, we made a particular effort to have interviewees refer us to those with the different views. These measures helped to enhance the representativeness of our sample. The sample's

members, we believe, provide the most comprehensive cata-
log ever assembled regarding the views of active armed robbers. Nevertheless, it must be emphasized that almost all of the
offenders we contacted were black, urban, and poor. Whether
our results can be generalized beyond that population is uncertain. Even if they cannot, the information we obtained
substantially expands our understanding of the crime of
armed robbery.

FIELD RELATIONS

We had to do more than find the offenders; we also had to
convince them to cooperate. This was easier said than done
because most of them were deeply suspicious of our motives.
We knew from our contact men that a number of the armed
robbers whom they approached refused to see us, despite
their best efforts to persuade them that we could be trusted.
That being so, why then were so many other offenders willing to talk to us?

The most obvious answer is that we paid them for their
participation. But this does not fully explain their cooperation. After all, these were individuals who were prepared to
take money by force without feeling compelled to provide
any service in return. Of course, unlike a stickup, participating in our project did not entail significant risk. But it must
be appreciated that, from the offenders' perspective, crime
probably appeared to be the safer option. Therein may lie
part of a paradoxical explanation. The perceived riskiness of
getting involved in our research clearly appealed to some of
the robbers, with the financial reward being little more than a
pleasant bonus.

Others agreed to participate no doubt only because one or
the other of our contact men convinced them that it was in
their interest to speak to us. These men did a remarkably good
job of selling our project. They employed several different
techniques to gain the cooperation of the offenders. Probably

the most successful was to point out to the robbers that they already were spending much of their time talking about crime with their associates on the street corner; here was a safer and more lucrative opportunity to recount their criminal exploits. Our field contacts often tried further to tempt the armed robbers by telling them that we planned to write a book based on our research. Many clearly were pleased by the prospect that what they had to say might be worthy of publication; they seemed to view this as a powerful acknowledgment of their street status and criminal expertise. Offenders are as likely as law-abiding citizens to desire social recognition for their competence; providing an avenue for such recognition can be a strong incentive for them to cooperate with researchers (West 1980).

Another strategy used by our contact men to convince offenders to participate in the project involved persuading them that talking to us would be therapeutic. Like most street criminals, the armed robbers we interviewed tended to lead problematic lives. It is testimony to the influence of pop psychology in our society that many of them, especially those heavily addicted to drugs, agreed to cooperate chiefly because they believed that speaking to professional social scientists might help them come to terms with their personal problems. It was not unusual for offenders to tell us at the close of interviews that they felt better for having gotten things off their chest; a few even said that they were going to make a concerted effort to give up drugs and go straight. To our knowledge, none managed to do so.

Sometimes our contact men simply asked the armed robbers to help us. Hardened street criminals often retain at least a limited capacity for prosocial behavior; some are prepared to assist friends, especially if they will be paid for their effort. Our field contacts felt that they knew some potential participants well enough to ask them to cooperate as a personal favor. On one occasion, for instance, we had arranged to take an offender to the scene of his most recent robbery. We arrived to find him busily engaged in selling crack on the street

corner; to our surprise, he immediately ceased his drug dealing and jumped into the car, saying, "Yeah, I'm making good
money today, but I told [the contact man] that I'd do this
for you."

Once offenders had agreed to see us, we took steps to put
them at ease during interviews. As a result of our earlier fieldwork with burglars, we had become familiar with the distinctive terminology and phrasing of street talk. We used that
knowledge to ask questions that were sensitive to how the
armed robbers spoke among themselves and thereby reduced
the likelihood of embarrassing breakdowns in communication. In speaking to the offenders, however, we did not try to be
one of them. As Hagedorn (1990:253) has cautioned, such attempts are doomed to failure: "Trying to act like an insider . . .
is phony, and the data reported inevitably will be phony."
Rather, we strove to create a comfortable interview situation
built on a foundation of shared meanings.

We also endeavored to make offenders comfortable by
honoring their requests for information about ourselves and
our project. A number of them, for example, asked us whether
we ever had committed a crime, and almost all had questions
about how the information they gave us would be used, who
would have access to it, and similar kinds of inquiries (see
Glassner and Carpenter 1985). We answered all of these questions straightforwardly, lest the offenders conclude that we
were being evasive. At the same time, we steadfastly refused
to answer questions concerning what other interviewees had
told us, explaining that the promise of confidentiality extended to everyone participating in our research. To have
done otherwise could only have undermined our trustworthiness and put the entire project in jeopardy.

A good deal has been written about the vulnerability of
criminological researchers to official coercion (see, e.g., Irwin
1972; McCall 1978; Polsky 1969). We recognized from the
outset the threat that intrusions from criminal justice authorities could pose to our project. The danger from police patrols
seemed especially great because we planned to visit the sites

of recent armed robberies with offenders. Therefore, prior to beginning our fieldwork, we negotiated a written agreement with the chief of the Saint Louis Metropolitan Police Department that his officers would not interfere in the conduct of the research. We carried a copy of this agreement with us at all times in the field but never had occasion to use it.

The project sometimes required us to put our personal safety at risk, and we had to adopt tactics to protect ourselves. We made a conscious effort to monitor and guard against potential dangers. The most obvious peril was that we ourselves might be robbed by our subjects. To keep that from happening, we let the offenders know that we carried little more cash than was necessary to pay them. We also were careful to keep other members of the research team apprised of where and with whom we were whenever we went onto the streets with offenders. Additionally, we visited recent offense sites only with subjects the project fieldworker regarded as especially "safe," that is, more stable and trustworthy than the rest. Even so, we were sufficiently worried about a couple of the subjects that we insisted on frisking them for weapons before letting them get into our car. It is better to be safe than sorry when working in volatile research settings, as Sluka (1990: 124) has noted: "One need not be paranoid about the dangers involved in doing research in violent social contexts, but a good dose of realistic appreciation goes a long way. And, all in all, it is no doubt better to be a bit paranoid about such things than it is to be a bit complacent about them."

We recognized that, scientifically speaking, restricting our site visits to the safest armed robbers was a less than ideal strategy. Given the potentially violent nature of our subject population, however, we felt that it would be foolhardy to do otherwise. As it turned out, even the most seemingly benign offenders were not always well behaved; during one site visit, for example, an offender leaned out of the car window and began flashing hand signs to rival gang members.

Another major threat to our safety was the possibility that offenders mistakenly would define us as police informants;

after all, we were asking them detailed questions regarding their involvement in serious crimes. To deal with this problem, we employed simple impression management techniques designed to allay suspicions about our motives (see, e.g., Berreman 1972; Sluka 1990). Whenever interviewees seemed to be uncomfortable with a line of questioning, we backed off and turned the conversation to other matters. We also were quick to respond to any fear expressed that we might be working for the police by denying that this was the case, showing them our university identification cards, and pointing out that many other offenders had talked to us without incident.

These strategies helped to mitigate the danger that "comes with the turf" in work with active violent criminals. But as Sluka (1990:124) has warned, "Danger is not a purely 'technical' problem and is never totally manageable." Despite our best efforts, we encountered a number of dangerous situations during the research period. Several offenders turned up for interviews carrying firearms. We occasionally were threatened with bodily injury by subjects who suddenly became angry or fearful. We nearly got caught in a gun battle between a drug dealer and a disgruntled customer. Probably the most nerve-racking situation arose when we scheduled two offenders for interviews at the same place and time, only to discover that one recently had robbed the other. Fortunately, we managed to hustle them off to separate locations before any trouble developed. The outcome could have been far different.

DATA COLLECTION AND ANALYSIS

Our semistructured interviews were tape-recorded, with the permission of each offender, as were the conversations during visits to the scenes of recent armed robberies. Only one of the interviewees objected to being taped; on that occasion, we took detailed notes. The tapes were transcribed verbatim, with identification tags inserted in the transcripts corresponding to relevant research issues. The tags permitted us, with the help of GOFER—a simple qualitative data software package—to retrieve comments made by the offenders about various predetermined matters. The issues that the tags covered generally were quite broad (e.g., motivation, victim selection). This left a great deal of scope for a more detailed analysis of cognitive and behavioral variations across offenses and offenders. We carried out this fine-grained analysis "by hand"; that is, we read the lists of comments and, for each issue, created categories that captured distinctions recognized by the offenders themselves as relevant.

The process of tagging interview transcripts usually is thought of as a precursor to formal data analysis. In reality, it represents an important analytical strategy in its own right. By tagging certain sorts of information and ignoring others, researchers effectively are deciding "what to tell and how to tell it" (Van Maanen 1988:25), since untagged data will not be readily available for further examination. The tagging decisions play a crucial role in determining the shape of the final narrative (see, e.g., Bennett 1981). Thus researchers must be explicit about the assumptions underlying their initial data reduction strategies.

Our tagging scheme reflected an interest in the mental processes involved in committing an armed robbery. We broke down the robbers' offenses into a series of distinct steps, or "sequential events" (Scheff 1990:195), that would allow us to explore objective and subjective aspects of the situation that influenced their decisions immediately before, during, and after their stickups. By examining what Katz (1988:3) calls the "foreground of criminality"—that is, the perceptual mechanisms through which offenses come to be contemplated and carried out—we sought to illuminate links between the lifestyles of the armed robbers and specific instances of lawbreaking. After all, criminal decision making does not take place in a vacuum; it is embedded in an "on-going process of human existence" (Bottoms and Wiles 1992:19).

Recent criminological theorizing has been dominated by rational choice explanations that overemphasize the extent to which offending is an independent, freely chosen action. The reality for many offenders is that crime commission has become so routinized that it emerges almost naturally in the course of their daily lives, often occurring without substantial planning or deliberation. This is what Hobbs (1995:4) means when he declares that the day-to-day activities associated with life on the street "are part of, not separate from, criminal action." The trick is to discover exactly how and why the day-to-day activities of offenders lead to crime. Only then might we be able to disrupt those activities before an offense is committed (see Cornish 1994).

In the chapters that follow we explore the decision-making strategies used by active armed robbers. Our focus, as noted earlier, is on features of the immediate situation that offenders take into account when contemplating and committing their stickups. The only way to see this process realistically, however, is to place it within the broader context of the offenders' lived experience; their decisions are shaped by everything from prevailing emotional states to internalized cultural forces. In keeping with the spirit of our analytical scheme, chapters have been arranged sequentially, taking the reader through the steps required to pull off a successful armed robbery. Chapter 2 examines the circumstances under which offenders become motivated to commit the offense, chapter 3 considers how and why they choose particular targets, and chapter 4 discusses the various tactics employed by offenders during the robbery event. The implications of our findings for crime prevention policy are explored in chapter 5.

Chapters 2, 3, and 4 make extensive use of quoted material from our conversations with the offenders. The quotations, of course, represent only a small portion of what our subjects told us. Selectivity is an unavoidable problem in the textual

representation of any aspect of social life, criminal or otherwise, and it would be naive to claim that this cannot distort
the resulting manuscript. As Bennett (1981:255) has cautioned, "A life is a life, but the representation of a life inevitably picks up some of its features from the representation
as well as from the life." In an effort to keep such distortion
to a minimum, we read parts of the evolving text to selected
members of our sample as the writing proceeded. This permitted us to check our interpretations against those of insid-
ers and to enlist their help in reformulating passages they regarded as misleading or inaccurate.

Two further caveats are in order. First, although we made
a concerted effort to question every offender about every issue, this was not always possible; in consequence, the number
of offenders responding to a question varies from one issue to
the next. For the major response categories, the number of
offenders speaking to the matter under scrutiny has been
noted. Second, to preserve their flavor and richness, quotations have not been edited to correct grammar, except where
this was necessary to make the meaning clear. Nor have these
quotations been censored; as a result, some readers may be
offended by certain words or passages. Bracketed text indicates the addition or substitution of a word or words. In-
dented quotations have been linked to the offenders responsible for them through the use of a self-assigned alias (given
only on the first occasion on which a particular robber is
quoted) plus a two-digit code number (see the appendix for
descriptive information on each respondent). Although the
aliases chosen by the offenders are presented without comment, we would urge the reader not to ignore them; many
provide significant insight into how our subjects view themselves and their social world.

2 Deciding to Commit an Armed Robbery

Official statistics tell us that arrested armed robbers are disproportionately young, poor, black, and male. It is tempting to read into such characteristics the mechanisms that drive offenders to commit stickups. After all, blacks who are young and poor have limited social and economic opportunities compared to older, more affluent whites. And it is part of our accepted wisdom that males are more violent and aggressive than females. But demography is not destiny. Many young, poor blacks never resort to any type of crime, let alone armed robbery. Conversely, some females regularly engage in predatory criminal violence. Demographic characteristics may identify a segment of the population as more likely than others to commit stickups, but such characteristics are not, and cannot be, causal agents. At most, they play an indirect role in facilitating such crimes by shaping the interactional environment within which potential offenders assess their current circumstances and prospects.

The direct cause of armed robbery is a perceptual process through which the offense comes to be seen as a means of meeting an immediate need, that is, through which a motive for the crime is formed. As Katz (1988:4) observes, demography notwithstanding, "something causally essential happens in the very moments in which a crime is committed. The assailant must sense, there and then, a distinctive constraint or seductive appeal that [was not sensed] a little while before in a substantially similar place." What are the causally essential constraints or appeals that underpin the decision to commit an armed robbery? That is the question to which the present chapter is devoted. Our goal is to understand the process whereby would-be armed robbers move from an unmotivated state to one in which they are determined to carry out a stickup.

With few exceptions, the decision to commit an armed robbery arises in the face of what offenders perceive to be a pressing need for cash (Conklin 1972; Gabor et al. 1987). Eighty of the eighty-one offenders in our sample who spoke directly to the issue of motivation said that they did stickups primarily because they needed money.

Being broke [gets me to thinking about doing an armed robbery] . . . cause being broke, man, you don't feel good. You ain't got nothing in your pocket, so you want to take something out of someone else's pocket. (Bill Williams—No. 78)

These offenders were not attempting to accumulate the capital necessary to achieve a long-range goal. They regarded money as the means to satisfy an immediate need. Armed robbery for them was a matter of day-to-day survival.

[The idea of committing an armed robbery] comes into your mind when your pockets are low; it speaks very loudly when you need things and you are not able to get what you need. It's not a want, it's things that you need, basic things that if you don't have the money, you have the artillery to go and get it. That's the first thing on my mind; concentrate on how I can get some more money. (Black—No. 79)

[Armed robbery] was a big joke more or less when I was younger. It ain't no joke now. It's survival. That's how I look at it now. (James Minor—No. 14)

Many of the offenders lurched from one financial crisis to the next. The frequency with which they committed armed robberies was governed largely by the amount of money in their pockets. Most appeared to give little thought to offending until they found themselves unable to meet current expenses.

[I commit an armed robbery] about every few months. There's no set pattern, but I guess it's really based on the need. If there is a period of time where there is no need of money . . . then it's not necessary to go out and rob. It's not like I do [stickups] for fun. (Slick Going—No. 04)

I can be sitting there, [not thinking about doing an armed robbery], and I might want to go somewhere and I might be broke. I only work part-time; so when I get paid and I give my people some money for staying with them, I'm [soon] broke again. So I might be sitting there and the thought might occur, "Well, if you gonna [commit a stickup], you'll have something [to spend] for a few days." So sometimes I might be idle and broke, might need some cigarettes or just need money in my pocket or one of my kids might call and need some money so I'll resort to my old way of getting [some]. (Bob Jones—No. 09)

Some offenders occasionally committed an armed robbery even though they had enough money to meet their immediate needs. By and large, the robberies that fell into this category were not for the purpose of improving the offenders' cash flow situation, but rather were the result of opportunities that seemed too good to pass up.

If I had five thousand dollars, I wouldn't do [an armed robbery] like tomorrow. But if I got five thousand dollars today and I seen you walking down the street and you look like you got some money in your pocket, I'm gonna take a chance and see. It's just natural. . . . If you see an opportunity, you take that opportunity. . . . It doesn't matter if I have five thousand dollars in my pocket, if I see you walking and no one else around and it look like you done went in the store and bought something and pulled some money out of your pocket and me or one of my partners has peeped this, we gonna approach you. That's just the way it goes. (John Brown— No. 47)

Among those who did not rob because of pressing financial need were several of the more successful commercial robbers, who tried never to let their cash reserves get too low;

they feared that the resulting financial desperation could cause them to take foolish risks. As one put it: "You've got to try to stay ahead. You don't want to have to do something and the time's not right." Staying ahead, however, was easier said than done because these offenders, like many others in our sample, were strongly committed to a hedonistic lifestyle that always threatened to exhaust their money supply. Typically, the armed robbers we spoke to did not save the cash derived through armed robbery; they used most or all of it to perpetuate a life of what we call "desperate partying."

DESPERATE PARTYING

A majority of the offenders in our sample spent much of the money they obtained through armed robbery to pursue what was for them an open-ended quest for excitement and sensory stimulation. Forty of the fifty-nine offenders who told us what they did with the proceeds of their stickups said they used most of the cash to initiate or sustain various forms of illicit action, including gambling, drug use, and heavy drinking.

I [have] a gambling problem and I . . . lose so much so I [have] to do something to [get the cash to] win my money back. So I go out and rob somebody. That be the main reason I rob someone. (Beano—No. 66)

I like to mix and I like to get high. You can't get high broke. You really can't get high just standing there, you got to move. And in order to move, you got to have some money. . . . Got to have some money, want to get high. (No. 14)

While the offenders often referred to such activities as partying, there is a danger in accepting this definition of the situation uncritically; the activities were pursued with an intensity and grim determination that suggest that something far more serious was at stake. For those in our sample, participation in illicit street action was no party, at least not in the conventional sense of the term. They appeared to find it anything but relaxing and showed little or no inclination to exercise the personal restraint that characterizes suburban cocktail parties. Rather, they gambled, used drugs, and drank alcohol heedless of any consequences. In the process, many of them began to contemplate their next stickup.

Katz (1988:198) argues that the successful integration of diverse illicit activities into a distinctive lifestyle plays a direct role in motivating persistent armed robbers to commit their offenses: "It is specifically the connection among the various forms of illicit action—the possibility of constructing a transcendent way of life around action—that sustains the motivation to do stick-ups." He interprets armed robbery as being viewed by offenders as little more than a game, just another way of "getting over" or "beating the odds." The offenders we interviewed, however, implied that the connection between armed robbery and other sorts of illicit action often was more subtle. Their motivation to commit a stickup emerged during a period of intense self-indulgence and from a growing sense of frustration and anger because they felt themselves to be locked into a cycle of events that was leading nowhere.

I'm walking around, sometimes if I have any money in my pocket I go get high, buy a bag of [marijuana], a forty-ounce [malt liquor] or something. Get high and then I ain't got no more money and then the highness makes you start thinking until you go out and do [a robbery]. It just makes me upset, angry, mad, jealous . . . cause I ain't got the stuff that [others] got. (Looney—No. 25)

[I think about armed robbery when] I need some money. I like money in my pocket, I like going out and getting drunk. When I get drunk, I get to tripping off shit that been happening with me, shit that been going through my life and shit [that] ain't right. And [doing stickups] is just how I get my satisfaction, I guess. Just go out and just do it. (Tony Brown—No. 81)

In such an emotional state, some of the offenders—especially the younger ones—are prone to interpret any display of wealth by others in their neighborhood as a personal affront that should not go unpunished. Often the punishment of choice is an armed robbery.

[What makes me suddenly decide to do a stickup is] being broke, thinking that you don't have no money . . . and then seeing all these other niggers driving a Lexus or something like that. They won't give you nothing. . . . There ain't no other way but to get 'em. (Big Prod—No. 46)

I do the people that drive they fancy cars and they be on they phones, they be high-catting, you know, like they got all this . . . them the ones I get. (Ne-Ne—No. 31)

None of this should be taken to suggest that the offenders are hapless victims of circumstance. Many of them voluntarily enter into the illicit activities that drive them toward lawbreaking. But their activities have a marked tendency to encapsulate them and isolate them from the influence of conventional others, so that they come to perceive themselves as having little choice but to continue robbing.

Why do the offenders find the open-ended pursuit of illicit action so seductive in the first place? The answer lies in their strong attachment to street culture. Street culture revolves around "the enjoyment of 'good times' with minimal concern for obligations and commitments that are external to the . . . immediate social setting" (Shover and Honaker 1992:283). To be seen as hip on the street, one must demonstrate an ability to make something happen now. There is no reputational mileage to be gained through deferred gratification. The offenders are easily seduced by street culture at least in part because they view their future prospects as bleak and see little point in long-range planning. Asked about his future plans, for example, one offender replied that there was no use thinking about such matters:

I really don't dwell on things like that. One day I might not wake up. I don't even think about what's important to me. What's important to me is getting mine [now]. (Kid Kutt—No. 59)

Participation in street culture represented an achievable source of personal identity that had the side benefit of helping to mask the offenders' "abiding sense of failure" (Kornhauser 1978:131). Few alternative sources of social support realistically were available to them, and many spent more time on the street corner than anywhere else. As one put it: "Basically, my whole life revolves around the street." During our interviews, we asked thirty-two of the offenders to tell us about their living arrangements; twenty-two said that they seldom slept at the same address for more than a few nights in a row, preferring to move from place to place as the mood struck them.

[I don't always stay at the same place.] I got a couple of little girlfriends and I'm just in and out, in and out. [I sleep at one address for] about two or three nights. Just got to move around. I don't like staying in one place all the time. (Carlos Reed—No. 64)

[I move around]; sometimes I stay on [a local street address], my brother and I have a home together out there. I have an ex-wife and kids on [another local street] and I stay there sometimes with them. . . . Then I have a room in my parents' house too. (W. Joe Murphy—No. 70)

I guess I'm just a street person, a roamer. I like to be out in the street. . . . Now I'm staying with a cousin. . . . That's where I live, but I'm very rarely there. I'm usually in the street. If somebody say they got something up . . . I go and we do whatever. I might spend the night at their house or I got a couple of girls I know [and] I might spend the night at their house. I'm home about two weeks out of a month. (Larry Pate—No. 71)

In effect, these offenders live as "urban nomads," ranging across the streets and alleys that connect the high-crime inner-city neighborhoods of Saint Louis (Stein and McCall 1994). These areas are the stamping grounds of the alienated, places dominated by dangerous and volatile losers for whom the code of the streets has replaced the conventional moral order (Anderson 1994). Lofland (1969) observes that the more time people spend in a deviant social setting, the more likely it is that they will embrace a deviant identity. Is it therefore any wonder that the offenders come to see their fate as inextricably linked to their ability to fulfill the imperatives of street culture?

Fulfilling the imperatives of life on the street is an expensive proposition. The relentless pursuit of action, whether in the form of heavy drinking, drug use, or high-stakes gambling, requires a great deal of money. The offenders in our sample seldom had enough cash in their pockets to sustain such activities for long. One seasoned armed robber explained to us that he had learned through experience never to embark on a session of illicit drug use without sufficient funds on hand; to do otherwise risked triggering a series of impulsive crimes, each designed to extend the session for a little bit longer.

[I commit armed robberies] mostly when I really *need* money or when I *want* some money. There is a difference between need and want. . . . I might *want* some money to buy me some drugs, then I might *need* some money to buy me some drugs when I'm really desperate. . . . I might go get eighty dollars [on a stickup]. Well, eighty dollars ain't gonna be no drugs. I know this cause I done been through this situation [before] and that's when I'm gonna [end up coming] back outside again and do the same thing. That starts a pattern. (Fred Harris—No. 74)

Even when the offenders had a substantial sum of money, their disdain for long-range planning coupled with their desire to live for the present often encouraged them to spend it with reckless abandon. The result was that they were under almost constant pressure to generate additional funds. That pressure, in turn, often led them to decide to commit an armed robbery. To the extent that the offense ameliorated their distress, it nurtured a tendency for them to view armed robbery as a reliable method of dealing with similar pressures in the future. In this way, the groundwork was laid for the continuation of their present street culture lifestyle. The self-indulgent activities of that culture inevitably precipitated new pressures. Thus a vicious cycle developed in which the offenders became increasingly desperate as they were drawn deeper and deeper into a way of life from which they saw little chance of escape.

KEEPING UP APPEARANCES

Of the fifty-nine offenders who identified their use of the money derived from armed robberies, fifteen reported that they purchased "status enhancing" items. Foremost among these was clothing; all fifteen said that, among other things, they always bought some clothes with the proceeds of their crimes. These offenders were not buying clothes simply to protect themselves from the elements, but rather to project a desired image; they sought to create a look of cool transcendence that suggested that they were members of the aristocracy of the streets.

You ever notice that some people want to be like other people? . . . They might want to dress like this person, like dope dealers and stuff like that. They go out there [on the street corner] in diamond jewelry and stuff. "Man, I wish I was like him!" You got to make some kind of money [to look like that], so you want to make a quick hustle. (Robert Lee Davis—No. 12)

Wearing the right clothes is an important part of fitting into any social setting. This is no less true for street culture, which has its own dress code. That code calls for the bold display of the latest status symbol clothing and accessories, a look that loudly proclaims the wearer to be someone who has overcome—if only temporarily—the financial difficulties faced by others on the street corner (Katz 1988).

Indeed, one female offender reported that she sometimes robbed people not for money but simply because she wanted their jewelry so she could flaunt it in front of others.

[Sometimes we commit armed robberies] just to get the jewelry and sport it around for a while. Sport it off for a while and, when [we] low on cash, pawn it in. (Janet Outlaw—No. 58)

In doing so, this offender was showing off in much the same manner that provoked some of the robbers to commit their stickups in the first place. As we have seen, it was not uncommon for offenders to tell us that they regarded people who engaged in such displays as deserving to be robbed. And a number of them acted on that perception. The irony is that often they then used the proceeds to behave in a similar fashion themselves.

I be out on the street, I be walkin' and I ain't got no money . . . and I see a nigger on my set that I don't know with a cool-ass car. . . . I feel I got to get his ass for his money and his motherfucking car. [Get his gold] chain or something on my neck, a cool ass-car, and be sporting around in [it] and shit. [But I] don't keep that motherfucker too long. (No. 31)

Shover and Honaker (1992:283) have argued that the intense concern of offenders with outward appearances, as with their notorious "partying," grows out of a strong attachment to the values of street culture, values that place great emphasis on the "ostentatious enjoyment and display of luxury items." A prominent part of being seen as "cool" on the street involves demonstrating that one has "made it" by flaunting the material trappings of success. Given the desperation that dominates the lives of the offenders in our sample, it is easy to appreciate why those who have made a lucrative score are anxious to show off their newly acquired possessions. But there is an obvious element of one-upmanship in doing so, and these offenders risk exposing themselves to the wrath of others who have not been so lucky (Anderson 1994). Processes such as this may help to explain the isomorphic relationship between offending and victimization (Lauritsen et al. 1991). Of the thirty offenders we asked about criminal victimization, twenty-four reported that they had been robbed at least once.

It would be misleading to suggest that the offenders differed markedly from their law-abiding neighbors in wanting to wear flashy clothes or drive a fancy car. Nor were all of their purchases ostentatious. For example, it was not unusual for them to use a portion of the proceeds of their stickups for a haircut or a manicure. What set the offenders apart from other people was their willingness to spend large amounts of cash on luxury items to the detriment of more pressing financial concerns. Katz (1988) has argued that for those who are committed to street culture, the reckless spending of money on expensive goods is an end in itself, demonstrating their disdain for the ordinary citizen's pursuit of financial security. Underlying such disdain is a self-centered and strongly predatory orientation to life. Why should one worry about money when more of it can be obtained so easily? One offender likened armed robbery to taking candy from a baby, adding "that's why we call it stick candy, cause it's sweet, you know . . . the more you do it, the easier it gets." But the free spending of the offenders further jeopardized their fiscal stability and left them with few alternatives except to continue committing crimes; keeping things together became a never-ending challenge.

KEEPING THINGS TOGETHER

While most of the offenders spent much of the money they acquired through armed robbery on illicit drugs and fashionable outfits, a substantial number also used some of it to cover daily living expenses. Nineteen of the fifty-nine offenders who specified a particular use for the proceeds of their crimes claimed that they needed the cash for necessities such as food, shelter, and child care products.

I don't think there is any one factor that precipitates the commission of a crime. . . . I think it's just the conditions. I think the primary factor is being without. Rent is coming up. A few months ago, the landlord was gonna put us out, rent due, you know. Can't get no money no way else. Ask family and friends, you might try a few other ways of getting the money, and as a last resort, I know I can go get some money [by committing an armed robbery]. (Tony Wright—No. o8)

Such claims conjure up an image of reluctant criminals doing the best they can to survive in circumstances not of their own making. In one sense, this image is not so far off the mark; certainly the offenders did not choose the socioeconomic arrangements into which they were born. In another sense, however, the contention that they are driven to crime by conditions entirely beyond their control strains credulity. All but a few of them routinely spent the majority of their funds on alcohol or drugs and used whatever happened to be left over to meet necessary expenses.

Many of the offenders complained bitterly about the constant pressure of bills; ten of them said that they paid bills with the cash generated by their stickups. Often, however, these bills were badly delinquent because the offenders disregarded them for as long as possible, even when they had the money, in favor of buying drugs. Typically, it was only when the threat of serious repercussions (e.g., being evicted, having the electricity or gas supply cut off) created unbearable pressure for the offenders that they relented and settled their accounts.

By me being involved with drugs, I keep a financial strain on myself. Unfortunate, but I do. . . . [I spend] the majority of [my money on drugs], unfortunately. Take care of the household as best I can, stay late in bills, but I manage to keep the light and gas on, rent paid, food; stay late, stay behind, and it's all because of drugs, basically. If it wasn't for drugs, I would be just doing what a normal person would do. I would probably be doing extremely well. (No. 70)

You are sitting there alone and you feeling light in your pocket, your rent is due, light and gas bill, you got these bill collectors sending you letters all the time, and you say, "I wish I had some

money. I need some money." Those are the haints. [You haint got
this and you haint got that.] Your mind starts tripping cause you
ain't got no money and the wolves are at the door. Can't be throwing no bread. . . . [After my last stickup] I gave my landlord some
money and sent a little money off to the electric company, a little
bit off to the gas company. I still had like twenty or thirty dollars in
my pocket. I got me some beer, some cigarettes, and [spent] some
on a stone [of crack cocaine]; enjoy myself for a minute. I let the
people know I'm trying to pay you and they ain't gonna be knock-
ing on my door. Now I can do me legitimate hustles until the
crunch comes again. (Ray Holmes—No. 76)

Since spontaneity is an enduring feature of street culture,
it is not surprising that the armed robbers often displayed a
strong determination to live for the moment. Indeed, Katz
(1988) suggests that, through careless spending, persistent
criminals seek to establish the conditions that will drive them
back to crime. Whether offenders spend money in a deliberate attempt to create such conditions is open to question; the
subjects in our sample gave no indication of doing so, appearing simply to be financially irresponsible. Whatever the explanation, the important point is that, consciously or not, the
offenders were largely the authors of their own destinies.
This is not to say that they freely chose to engage in armed
robbery through a process of careful calculation. Rather, their
behavior had a nasty way of placing them under the gun to
obtain cash as quickly as possible. One offender, for instance,
told us that he had committed ten armed robberies in the past
month because he needed to pay his private attorney; he was
awaiting trial on an aggravated assault charge and did not
want to take his chances with a public defender. Another offender reported that he was doing stickups to "reestablish"
himself after serving a lengthy prison sentence for armed
robbery.

The overall picture that emerges is one of people caught
up in a cycle of expensive, self-indulgent habits that feed on
themselves and constantly call for more of the same (Lemert
1953). It would be a mistake to conclude that the offenders
are being driven to crime by genuine financial hardship; few

of them are doing stickups to buy the proverbial loaf of bread to feed their children. At the same time, though, most of their crimes are economically motivated. The offenders perceive themselves as needing money and their offenses typically are a response to that perception.

WHY ROBBERY?

The decision to commit an armed robbery, then, usually is motivated by a perceived need for cash. But why does this need express itself as armed robbery? Presumably the offenders have other means of obtaining money. Why do they choose armed robbery over legitimate work? Why do they decide to commit a stickup instead of borrowing the money from a friend or relative? And why do they select armed robbery rather than some other crime?

That the decision to commit an armed robbery typically emerges in the course of illicit street action suggests that legitimate employment does not represent a realistic solution for most of the offenders in our sample; the immediacy of their need for cash effectively rules out work as a viable money-making strategy. In any case, the jobs available to these offenders—almost all of them unskilled and poorly educated—pay wages that fall far short of being able to support their cash-intensive activities.

Education-wise, I fell late on the education. I just think it's too late for that. They say it's never too late, but I'm too far gone for that. . . . I've thought about [getting a job], but I'm too far gone, I guess. . . . I done seen more money come out of [doing stickups] than I see working. (Wyman Danger—No. 02)

Minimum wage is four dollars and twenty-five cents. You work forty hours. By the time they take out taxes and then most places you have to wait two weeks to see two-hundred dollars, and then you got to wait two more weeks. I'm not saying that it's right for me to do what I'm doing, but I'm so used to the easy way [of getting money]. (No. 09)

Beyond this, a small number of the offenders rejected the idea of legitimate employment altogether, claiming that a job would cramp their lifestyle.

I'm a firm believer, man, God didn't put me down on this earth to suffer for no reason. I'm just a firm believer in that. I believe I can have a good time every day, each and every day of my life, and that's what I'm trying to do. I never held a job. The longest job I ever had was about nine months . . . at Saint Louis Car; that's probably the longest job I ever had, outside of working in the joint. But I mean on the streets, man, I just don't believe in [work]. There is enough shit on this earth right here for everybody, nobody should have to be suffering. You shouldn't have to suffer and work like no dog for it, I'm just a firm believer in that. I'll go out there and try to take what I believe I got coming [because] ain't nobody gonna walk up . . . and give it to me. [I commit stickups] because I'm broke and need money; it's just what I'm gonna do. I'm not going to work! That's out! I'm through [with work]. I done had twenty-five or thirty jobs in my little lifetime [and] that's out. I can't do it! I'm not going to! (No. 14)

I can't work. I don't want to work. I don't have time to wait on nothing coming to me every week or every two weeks. (Wallie Cleaver—No. 48)

One offender pointed out that armed robbery was much easier than working for a living.

[Armed robbery is] not boring, it gets good. The money, as far as paying bills and stuff like that, [robbery is] much easier [compared to] working. It's just like you been living the hustler type of life . . . and that's just the kind of life we make, that's just it, [we want easy money]. (John Lee—No. 13)

And another added that, having spent many years in prison, he no longer had the time to earn his way to the top through legitimate employment; his only realistic chance of achieving financial security was to pull off a string of lucrative crimes.

After a certain age, you know, you may get a few [legitimate] jobs, this and that, but if you been in jail and this and that, you really

want something quicker. You don't want to just lay around and
work now, you just want to make some quick money and get some
stuff together, get you some cars, get you a house. You want to do
this as quick as possible. You don't want to lay around and try to
work no twenty years. And you gonna be up in age as it is, so . . .
(No. 12)

The "conspicuous display of independence" is a bedrock
value on which male street corner culture rests (Shover and
Honaker 1992:284); to be seen as cool one must always do as
he pleases. This cultural ethos often brings members into con-
flict with the demands of legitimate employment because employees are expected to do as they are told by the boss. Certainly crime appealed to some of the offenders in our sample
precisely because it allowed them to flaunt their independence from the routine imposed by the world of work.

Perhaps not surprisingly, most of the offenders who said
they were unwilling to work for a living were experienced
armed robbers with long criminal records; they recognized
that the only jobs available to them were menial with little or
no chance for advancement. Crime, on the other hand, possessed an entrepreneurial edge that allowed them to gain "a
measure of respect, if not from others, at least from [them-
selves]" (Shover and Honaker 1992:288).

I don't like working, really, just mainly for myself because, really,
this isn't a racist thing, it's just kind of a personal thing with people
telling me what to do. . . . I spent so much time in the penitentiary,
and being on a [legitimate] job seems like it's a problem [for me].
(Cedric Rhone—No. 05)

From their perspective, then, why should these offenders subordinate their immediate desires to the requirements of a job
that they see both as demeaning and as holding no promise for
the future?

Nevertheless, many of the offenders reported that they
wanted lawful employment; twenty-five of the seventy-five
unemployed subjects who said that they did stickups mostly

for the money claimed they would stop committing offenses if someone gave them a "good" job.

> My desire is to be gainfully employed in the right kind of job. . . . If I had a union job making sixteen or seventeen dollars [an hour], something that I could really take care of my family with, I think that I could become cool with that. Years ago I worked at one of the [local] car factories; I really wanted to be in there. It was the kind of job I'd been looking for. Unfortunately, as soon as I got in there they had a big layoff. (Robert Gibson—No. 69)

> I would take a job paying six dollars an hour, something like that. I'll work, it's cool. Ain't nothing wrong with working for real. If I get a little bitty job . . . I wouldn't have to be out in these streets robbing people. I'm cool. Get a little [house], find a little girl to settle down. I don't want to be rich. Buy a little thirty-thousand-dollar house, something like that. (Andrew—No. 44)

And a few others admitted that, while a job probably would not eliminate their offending altogether, it might well slow them down.

> [If a job were to stop me from committing stickups], it would have to be a straight-up good-paying job. I ain't talking about no six dollars an hour. . . . I'm talking like ten to eleven dollars an hour, something like that. But as far as five or six dollars an hour, no! I would have to get like ten or eleven dollars an hour, full-time. Now, something like that, I would probably quit doing [stickups]. I would be working, making money, I don't think I would do it no more. I wouldn't actually quit; I don't know [that] I would quit altogether. It would probably slow down and then eventually I'll stop. I think [my offending] would slow down. (No. 58)

While such claims may or may not be sincere, it is unlikely that they ever will be challenged. Attractive employment opportunities are limited for all inner-city residents, and the vast majority of the offenders are not well placed to compete for the few good jobs available. Most of them realized this and, with varying degrees of bitterness, were resigned to being out of work.

I fill out [job] applications daily. Somebody [always] says, "This is bad that you got tattoos all over looking for a job." In a way, that's discrimination. How do they know I can't do the job? I could probably do your job just as well as you, but I got [these jailhouse] tattoos on me. That's discriminating. Am I right? That's why most people rob and steal because, say another black male came in like me [for a job], same haircut, same everything. I'm dressed like this, tennis shoes, shorts, and tank top. He has on [a] Stacy Adams pair of slacks and a button-up shirt with a tie. He will get the job before I will. That's being racist in a way. I can do the job just as well as he can. He just dresses a little bit better than me. (Antwon Wright— No. 56)

Even if the offenders were to land a high-paying job, it is doubtful that they would keep it for long. As Shover and Honaker (1992) have pointed out, the relentless pursuit of street action has a powerful tendency to undermine any commitment to conventional activities. In particular, the heavy use of psychoactive substances promoted by street corner culture often ensnares participants so that they begin to neglect the demands of legitimate employment in favor of enjoying the moment. As a result, they quickly find themselves out of work and desperate to locate other sources of income to maintain their increasing dependence on drugs and alcohol. Davis (1995) has called attention to the powerful part played by addictive drugs in blocking job opportunities for the inner-city poor; for those caught up in street life, he warns, "drug use is the padlock on the exit door."

In theory, the offenders perhaps could have borrowed some cash from a friend or relative rather than resorting to crime. In practice, however, this was not a feasible option. Most of them long ago had exhausted the patience and goodwill of others; not even their closest friends or family members were willing to loan them more money.

I can't borrow the money. Who gonna loan me some money? Ain't nobody gonna loan me no money. Shit, [I use] drugs and they know [that] and I rob and everything else. Ain't nobody gonna loan

me no money. If they give you some money, they just give it to
you; they know you ain't giving it back. (No. 02)

Besides, some of the male offenders were reluctant to keep
asking for loans because they believed that men should be self-
sufficient.

I don't like always asking my girl for nothing because I want to let
her keep her own money. . . . I'm gonna go out here and get some
money. (Treason Taylor—No. 77)

In any case, borrowing money offers only a short-term solution to financial difficulties. The expectation that loans will be
repaid in itself can trigger an armed robbery. As one offender
told us, "I have people that will loan me money, [but] they
will loan me money because of the work that I do; they know
they gonna get their money [back] one way or another."
Putting it bluntly, offenders who are unemployed and caught
up in heavy gambling, drinking, or drug use are not going to
solve their money troubles by borrowing additional cash, and
they know it.

When confronted with an immediate need for money,
then, the offenders in our sample perceive themselves as having little hope of getting cash quickly and legally. As Lofland
(1969) has observed, many of the most efficient solutions to
financial problems are against the law. But this does not explain why the subjects decided to carry out an armed robbery
instead of some other crime. Most of them had committed a
wide range of offenses in the past, and some continued to do
so. Why do they choose armed robbery?

For many of the offenders, this question was irrelevant;
armed robbery was their "main line," and alternative crimes
were not considered when the need for money arose.

[W]hen I was coming up, the people that I used to be around,
[armed robbery] was all they used to do. I guess I learned how to
do it the way they showed me, and that's really the only thing I
know how to do. (Lisa Wood—No. 83)

I have never been able to steal, even when I was little and they would tell me just to be the watch-out man. . . . Shit, I watch out, everybody gets busted. I can't steal, but give me a pistol and I'll go get some money. . . . [Armed robbery is] just something I just got attached to. (No. 13)

When these offenders did commit another kind of crime, it typically was prompted by the chance discovery of an especially vulnerable target.

I do [commit other sorts of offenses], but that ain't—I might do a burglary, but I'm jumping out of my field. See, I'm scared when I do a burglary [or] something like that. I feel comfortable robbing . . . but I see something they call "real sweet," like a burglary where the door is open and ain't nobody there or something like that, well . . . (No. 02)

Most of the offenders who expressed a strong preference for armed robbery had come to the offense through burglary, drug selling, or both. They claimed that doing stickups had several advantages over these other crimes. A number of them pointed out that armed robbery took much less time than breaking into buildings or dealing drugs; not only could the offense be committed more quickly, but it also typically netted cash rather than goods and thus avoided the delays inherent in disposing of hot merchandise.

I tried the drug [selling] thing for a minute, but the money wasn't coming right; it was too slow. I don't know, I give this man one-hundred dollars for a gram [and] I get back two-hundred dollars. But that's two-hundred dollars in like two days, where I [can] go look for somebody and rob them and get a grand in a day, in an hour. So the dope [dealing] thing ain't nothing. With robbery, it's just fast. (No. 31)

Robbery is the quickest money. Robbery is the most money you gonna get fast. . . . Burglary, you gonna have to sell the merchandise and get the money. Drugs, you gonna have to deal with too many people, [a] bunch of people. You gonna sell a fifty-dollar or hundred dollar bag to him, a fifty-dollar or hundred-dollar bag to him, it takes too long. But if you find where the cash money is and

just go take it, you get it all in one wad. No problem. I've tried burglary, I've tried drug selling . . . the money is too slow. (No. 70)

Some of the offenders who favored armed robbery over other
crimes maintained that the offense also was safer than burglary or dope dealing.

I feel more safer doing a robbery because doing a burglary, I got a
fear of breaking into somebody's house not knowing who might be
up in there. I got that fear about house burglary. . . . On robbery I
can select my victims, I can select my place of business. I can watch
and see who all work in there or I can rob a person and pull them
around in the alley or push them up in a doorway and rob them.
You don't got [that] fear of who . . . in that bedroom or somewhere
in another part of the house. (Melvin Walker—No. 01)

Burglary, there is always that element of surprise. You can crawl
through somebody's window and they be waiting on you and send
you right back out. You never know what's in that house waiting
on you. Robbery, it's just you and that individual out in the open.
(No. 09)

If I'm out there selling dope, somebody gonna come—and I'm not
the only one out there robbing, you know—so somebody like me,
they'll come and rob me. . . . I'm robbing cause the dope dealers is
the ones getting robbed and killed, you know. (No. 48)

And quite a few of them said that armed robbery was less of
a threat to their freedom as well.

If you sell drugs, it's easy to get locked up selling drugs; plus, you
can get killed selling drugs. You get killed more faster doing that.
(Vincent Ray—No. 16)

Robbery you got a better chance of surviving and getting away
than doing other crimes. . . . You go break in a house, [the police]
get the fingerprints, you might lose a shoe, you know how they got
all that technology stuff. So I don't break in houses. . . . I leave that
to some other guy. (No. 59)

My style is, like, [I] don't have to be up in nobody's house in case
they come in; they might have a pistol in the house or something.

It's easier to get caught [too because you can] leave fingerprints or anything in that type of business. But when you robbing somebody that's selling drugs, that's different. They ain't going to the police. (No. 66)

Several offenders told us that increased law enforcement activities aimed at curbing street corner drug sales in Saint Louis had caused them to switch from dope dealing to armed robbery.

Why not sell drugs? Because the people you sell drugs to might be undercover police. We've slowed down drugs a little and started robbing people. . . . My friend that I been robbing people with, he sold drugs to a detective; a dude he trusted set him up. So we stopped selling drugs and we going into robbery. (Thugg—No. 42)

Finally, a couple of the armed robbers reported that they had learned to steer clear of dope selling because their strong craving for drugs made it too difficult for them to resist their own merchandise.

It's not good for me to be around [drugs]. I'm not a strong-willed person where I can handle something that I used to love and [still] profit from it. I would become my best customer. (No. 09)

I think robbery is more easier. . . . A dope fiend can't be selling dope because he be his best customer. I couldn't sell dope [nowadays]. I could sell a little weed or something cause I don't smoke too much of it. But selling rock [cocaine] or heroin, I couldn't do that cause I mess around and smoke it myself. [I would] smoke it all up! (No. 78)

Without a doubt, some of the offenders in our sample were prepared to commit crimes other than armed robbery; they wanted money quickly and could not afford to be choosy about how they got it. More often than not, however, these offenders elected to do a stickup because this appeared to be the "most proximate and performable" (Lofland 1969:61) offense available to them. The universe of moneymaking crimes from which they realistically could pick was fairly limited. By and large, they did not hold jobs that would allow them to violate even a low-level position of financial trust. Nor did they possess the technical know-how to commit lucrative commercial break-ins or the interpersonal skills needed to perpetrate successful frauds. Even street corner dope dealing was unavailable to many of them; they lacked the financial wherewithal to get started. Indeed, several interviewees reported that they sometimes did stickups as a means of generating the cash necessary to finance their drug selling.

Sometimes we fall off when we sell dope; sometimes we lose our dope. Sometimes the police take our dope and don't lock us up. In our neighborhood, we got this policeman and he'll take our dope and our money and just send us on our way. He'll keep the money and the dope; [the police are] crooked like that. So we have to do another [armed robbery] or something to get back on our feet. (Taz—No. 52)

Thus, in times of financial desperation, the offenders had only a few viable alternatives to armed robbery, crimes such as theft (typically shoplifting), car stealing, or residential burglary. And they knew through experience that, other things being equal, doing a stickup represented the most efficient solution to their current troubles. This is the insight that separates persistent armed robbers from their street corner peers; for those who can stomach the violence, doing stickups seems so much easier than other types of hustling that it becomes increasingly more difficult to contemplate alternative crimes.

[Robbery] is just easy. I ain't got to sell no dope or nothing, I can just take the money. Just take it, I don't need to sell no dope or work. . . . I don't want to sell dope, I don't want to work. I don't feel like I need to work for nothing. If I want something, I'm gonna get it and take it. I'm gonna take what I want. . . . If I don't have money, I like to go and get it. I ain't got time [for other offenses]; the way I get mine is by the gun. I don't have time to be waiting on people to come up to me buying dope all day. . . . I don't have time for that, so I just go and get my money. (No. 48)

The bottom line is that the offenders, when faced with a pressing need for cash, tend to resort to armed robbery because they know that no other course of action, legal or otherwise, offers as quick and easy a way out of their financial difficulties. Lofland (1969:50) has observed that most people, when under pressure, have a tendency to become fixated on removing the perceived cause of that pressure "as quickly as possible." Those in our sample were no exception to this rule. In a desperate state, they were not predisposed to consider unfamiliar, complicated, or long-term solutions (see Lofland 1969:50–54) and instead turned to armed robbery, which they knew well. This often seemed to happen almost automatically, the stickup emerging out of a more general path of illicit action (e.g., partying) with minimal calculation. The cold-blooded rationality popularly attributed to armed robbers was a scarce commodity among the offenders we interviewed.

THE SEDUCTIONS OF ARMED ROBBERY

Katz (1991:300) has argued that persistent armed robbers are motivated less by the need for money than by a desire to transcend "the omnipresent threat of chaos in contemporary, urban, street criminal life." In committing stickups, Katz asserts, offenders are seeking to exploit their potential for violence as a means of exerting ruthless control over their surroundings. We found little evidence in our research to support Katz's contention that the primary motivation for armed robbery is psychic rather than financial. Only one offender we talked to—a woman—said that for her the emotional benefits of the offense typically had more causal force than the potential monetary reward; each of this person's four previous stickups was motivated by a desire to get even with someone who had wronged her.

Though only one offender reported becoming motivated primarily by the psychic rewards of armed robbery, a number of them viewed such rewards as an important secondary benefit of the crime. Several of those who did stickups mostly to raise cash added that they enjoyed dominating their victims and got a great kick out of frightening them.

The money is the point [of robbery], that's all. [But] pulling the gun, watching they face, how scared they get and all that . . . that's fun too. (K-Money #2—No. 60)

This might sound stupid, but I [also] like to see a person get scared, be scared of the pistol. . . . You got power. I come in here with a big old pistol and I ain't playing. . . . You gonna do [what I say]. I like [robbery] cause you got the power and, like I said, it's a quick way of getting money. (Rudy—No. 10)

Others who committed armed robberies chiefly for monetary reasons said that such offenses also gave them an opportunity to take charge of their daily lives.

I make it happen [through robbery]. There is only three types of people in this world: those that wonder what happen; those that know what happen; and then people like me that make shit happen. I make happen whatever I want to happen. (Frank Nitti #2— No. 63)

[On one of my armed robberies] me and a friend of mine . . . was standing up over [the victims] with these big old guns and these people were saying, "Take the money! Take the money! Just don't shoot us!" I didn't have any intentions of shooting anybody any- way. But I'm just saying that when a person is telling me that, you [are] in control. You can either take their life like that or you can just let them live. That's what it is, a control thing . . . you suc- ceeded in having the authority to control people. You think about it and you say, "I had this much control in my hands." Really, it's an unexplainable thing. (Bennie Simmons—No. 07)

These offenders came closest to the armed robbers described by Katz in that, beyond cash, they got a sense of control out of their stickups as well. Remember that, by any conven- tional measure of success, virtually all of the offenders we in- terviewed were miserable failures, and they were well aware of this. Among the moneymaking crimes available to them, therefore, armed robbery was especially appealing because the successful completion of such a potentially dangerous offense represented "a thrilling demonstration of personal competence" (Katz 1988:9).

Beyond competence and control, some of the offenders who were motivated predominately by financial pressures said that they liked the violence inherent in the crime.

I been brought up around violence all my life. I done went to a psychiatrist when I was like seventeen, my mother was wondering why I was so violent. . . . I'm just violent. I just love to fight. . . . You say what makes [robbery] different [from other crimes]? A burglary, I feel like a burglary is nonviolent; you don't want to hurt anyone. It's like creeping in the dark. But I'm gonna do what I got to do to make ends meet. I don't want to try to tiptoe in and steal something. I'll just take it away from them. (No. 63)

One subject reported that he found armed robbery particularly seductive because the offense allowed him to beat money out of his victims. As he put it: "It just be fun when we do the robbery cause we'll beat the person's ass bad, make 'em suffer. It just be so fun." Herein may lie an important difference between persistent armed robbers and other street corner hustlers. The armed robbers we spoke with typically displayed far more anger and hostility than the active residential burglars who took part in our earlier study (Wright and Decker 1994). Even in casual conversations, their strong propensity for sudden violence seemed to lurk just below the surface (see also Katz 1991).

We try not to kill [our victims]. If we can avoid killing them, then we try not to. But if they force your hand, then you have to kill them. It's just that simple. (No. 81)

In addition, a number of the offenders who usually resorted to armed robbery out of financial desperation occasionally committed the offense to get even with someone for a real or imagined wrong, for "revenge." One offender told us that he had robbed a group of drug dealers the day before because they had sold him "bad drugs." He claimed that he had not been especially short of cash at the time, but that he wanted to punish the dealers for mistreating him.

> They shouldn't do their customers like that. I feel like I'm out there taking a chance, risking my life to get the money [to buy drugs]. They should show me some respect. I'm making them rich; they shouldn't be so disrespectful. (No. 01)

Other offenders also described stickups perpetrated in the name of a rough and ready form of street justice (see Black 1983). The purest example of such a robbery was provided by a parolee who, because he denied being a currently active offender, was not included in our sample. Nevertheless, we spoke to him at some length. He recently had been released from prison, where he had served several years for robbing someone to collect on a bad debt. He explained that he had not intended to rob the person but had acted impulsively because he was sick and tired of being taken for a sucker.

> I've only done one robbery, and to me it wasn't a robbery, but that's how [the authorities] rated it. I had loaned a guy some money and I was kinda down on my luck or whatever. I used to ask this guy for my money, and he would always tell me that he didn't have it. But he was working every day! This particular day here, I seen him with some money. In fact, he'd just cashed his check or whatever and I asked for my money and he said that he didn't have any money. So really, I just took what he owed me, and that was about sixty dollars. I took that from him. I did not take all the money he had, I just took the sixty dollars that he owed me and gave him back the rest of his money. Well, I throwed it on the ground and I know he got it back. But he told the police that he was robbed and I went to prison for it. Well, basically it was a robbery because he didn't consent for me to have the money; he didn't say willingly that I could have it. I told him that if he didn't give me the money I was gonna kill him. But in my way of thinking that's how I deal with it. I was just fed up.

Armed robbery, as noted in chapter 1, often is an interracial event in which a white victim is confronted by a black assailant. This raises a question as to whether such crimes are racially motivated. To be sure, a majority of the black offenders in our sample routinely robbed whites; some even expressed a strong preference for white victims. But none of these offenders indicated that they were motivated to rob whites specifically by racial hatred. In fact, only two of the interviewees admitted to disliking whites, and neither of them had ever robbed one. That said, the offenders, especially the males, frequently used vicious racial epithets during stickups, though their black victims were every bit as likely as their white ones to be subjected to such abuse. Armed robbers are not politically correct; racial putdowns are part and parcel of their everyday speech and, as we shall see in chapter 4, find ready expression during robberies.

SUMMARY

The offenders in our study typically decide to commit their armed robberies while under what they perceive to be intense financial pressure to sustain various forms of illicit action (e.g., gambling, drug use, and heavy drinking). Studies based on incarcerated armed robbers also have concluded that most stickups are motivated by a perceived need for money. What those studies have missed, however, is that the offenders' financial desperation is linked inextricably to their intense involvement in the self-indulgent activities promoted by street culture. Farrington (1993) suggests that offenders' claims that they were driven to crime by a lack of money could be tested simply by giving them cash and observing whether or not their offending decreased. Our hypothesis, on the basis of street-based research, would be quite the opposite; we would predict that giving money to the armed robbers would set off a round of drinking and drug taking that would plunge them deeper into financial desperation and thereby *increase* their lawbreaking.

That the armed robbers, at the time of actually contemplating their stickups, typically perceive themselves to be in a situation of immediate need has at least two important implications for real-world offender decision making. First, it suggests a mind-set in which they are seeking less to maximize their gains than to deal with a present crisis. Second, it indicates an element of desperation that probably weakens the influence of threatened sanctions and neutralizes any misgivings about the morality of taking someone else's possessions by force. This might help to explain why, even though the vast majority of incarcerated criminals report that armed robbery is not worth the risk (Figgie International 1988), many of them return to offending after release. Prison inmates are removed from the temptations and pressures of life on the street and therefore may calculate the risks and rewards of crime quite differently than they do on the outside. It is only through studying active offenders that we can gain a realistic understanding of the emotional and cultural forces that motivate their criminality.

3 Choosing the Target

Once offenders have decided to commit an armed robbery, they confront the task of selecting a promising target. This can be a complicated exercise. The offenders typically are seeking to solve a pressing financial problem as quickly as possible so they can resume their partying. At the same time, many of them are reluctant to do a stickup without first determining the likely risks and rewards. As the offenders attempt to settle on a robbery target, therefore, they are buffered by two seemingly conflicting demands: one calling for immediate action, the other counseling caution. How do they manage to reconcile these demands and choose a specific target? That is the question that this chapter seeks to answer. Our aim is to look at the target selection process in terms of the wider context of the lifestyles and daily activities of the offenders.

STREET ROBBERY

Offenders do not choose their robbery targets in a vacuum; their decisions are circumscribed by emotional states on one side and by sociocultural conditions on the other. Most of the armed robbers in our sample did not pick their targets in a calm, deliberate manner, but rather in a state of perceived desperation. In the throes of such a state, they were not inclined to weigh carefully the pros and cons of each target objectively available to them. Instead, the targets selected by the offenders often emerged as a result of their involvement in other forms of illicit street action. Katz (1991:297) noted a similar phenomenon in his study of persistent armed robbers, concluding that the "interlocking, open-ended . . . illicit activities" that constitute the essence of street life have a powerful tendency to bring offenders face to face with criminal opportunities. Not only does an intense commitment to drug taking, gambling, or prostitution bring a robber into frequent contact with vulnerable victims, but it also encourages a willingness to exploit their vulnerability.

I'm hanging out in the street on the corner [and] I'm always looking for a way to make some money. Always. And by me being right there, it's like an accident waiting to happen. . . . I don't look for [the target], it comes up. (No. 04)

Criminal Victims

Six out of every ten offenders in our sample who specialized in street robbery—forty-three of seventy-three—said that they usually preyed on individuals who themselves were involved in lawbreaking. Armed robberies against victims who are themselves criminals seldom show up in official crime statistics because they are unlikely to be reported to the police. As a result, they typically are excluded from studies of target selection in robbery, most of which are based on prison interviews (Katz 1991). Nevertheless, these offenses are important; they make a substantial contribution to the violent reputation of many so-called high-crime neighborhoods, and they play a crucial role in shaping the social environment within which a variety of illicit transactions are conducted. Moreover, to some extent such robberies may fuel official rates of serious criminal violence; some may result in injuries or deaths that cannot easily be covered up, and some may have a contagious effect whereby innocent victims also are targeted (see Loftin 1986).

Given that many of the offenders we spoke to had decided to commit their stickups so they could get high or stay high, it should come as no surprise that, of the forty-three who usually chose criminal victims, thirty-five said they preferred to rob dope dealers. Almost all of these offenders targeted young, street-level dealers who sold small quantities of crack cocaine directly to consumers. A few, however, sometimes robbed major drug suppliers whose illicit transactions were conducted several steps removed from the street corner. Part of the attraction of robbing dope dealers was that it was an efficient way to obtain drugs without having to pay for them. As one offender told us: "After I robbed my first dope dealer, I suddenly discovered that I didn't need any money to cop my drugs." Perhaps even more attractive, though, was drug dealers' tendency to use cash to transact their business.

[I like robbing] them drug dealers [because] it satisfies two things for me: my thirst for drugs and the financial aspect. [I can] actually pay my rent, pay for my car, [and things like that too.] (Marko Maze—No. 03)

[If you see a drug dealer] on the set, if you know how the set going, what's happening on the set, a lot of action on the set, you know he gonna have some money. . . . Either he got some money or he got something in his pocket that's gonna make some money. I can use that too. (No. 64)

[Dope men are perfect victims] cause they have all the money on them. . . . They carry all they money, jewelry, and all that on them, and all they drugs. (No. 25)

Recall that the offenders spend most of their time in neighborhoods marked by the open selling and use of illicit drugs. Street corner dope dealers are a prominent feature of the social landscape and part of their daily lives. Their tendency to prey on drug sellers also is facilitated by widespread resentment toward such people for the havoc wrought by drugs in inner-city neighborhoods.

[Drug dealers] ain't doing nothing but destroying lives, that's all. I seen drugs ruin too many people's lives and take too many people's lives. [Drug dealers] ruined my life, my family life, you know. I don't have no sympathy for drug dealers. (No. 03)

Those people, those drug dealers, they're not working-class people; they're a drain on society, and in a few more years they gonna have them all off the streets anyway. I've had police tell me that they wish they were all dead for real because they poisoning the street. I kind of look at me and a few other dudes that do this type of stuff and we are really helping the police for real. That's a crazy way of thinking about it, but [dope sellers] are causing more harm than people like me that just prey on drug dealers. . . . I'm taking from the dregs of society, parasites, which really they are because they don't give a flying fuck about me or my kids or your kids. They will pass that poison right to them and know it's gonna kill them. (No. 07)

These offenses can be carried out more or less on the spur of the moment because the offenders are familiar with their intended victims and know where to find them. As one explained, "I don't really look for drug dealers, they're just there."

A further benefit of robbing drug dealers, of course, is that such people were unlikely to turn to the police for help.

That's all I done robbed is drug dealers . . . they not gonna call the police. What they gonna tell the police? He robbed me for my dope? They is the easiest bait to me. I don't want to harm no innocent people, I just deal basically with drug dealers. (No. 63)

Nor were drug customers anxious to call attention to their activities by reporting to the police that they had been robbed. Thus they too were regarded as particularly good targets by some of the armed robbers in our sample. The offender quoted below, for example, often targeted white drug users when they entered high-crime black neighborhoods in search of cocaine. He reasoned that whites would have an especially difficult time explaining their presence in such areas.

[The perfect place to rob a white person is] in an all-black area with
a lot of crime. . . . [White] people that get robbed ain't supposed to
be there anyway cause they know what's going on and you taking
a chance. You know the consequences or the risks you taking when
you coming to buy some dope. Anything can happen . . . cause they
not supposed to be in the hood, period. Police don't want them
in there either cause they know they gonna get robbed. . . . I see
somebody white, that's payday. They in the wrong, man; they know
they in the wrong. . . . I rob somebody [white] going to get some
dope, I ain't gonna get caught, man. They can't tell [on you].
(K.C.—No. 86)

Few social settings are more anomic than the world of
street corner drug transactions, where an ability to mind one's
own business is regarded as a crucial survival skill. From the
offenders' perspective, this made such settings ideal for stickups; bystanders are disinclined to get involved and witnesses
are reluctant to make a police report.

When you are robbing drug dealers, the area is normally infested
with people, in and out, in and out. So [the dealers] don't have time
to look at everybody that's coming up on them. I would catch them
in a situation where they might have just got through handing
some drugs off and putting the money in their pocket. As the people
who have just bought the drugs are leaving, that's when I would get
[the dealers]. . . . Other people would see this going on, but it's
none of they business, they just keep on going. The basic drug
dealer, he doesn't [ply his trade in the best part of town]. I wouldn't
have to worry about being downtown and some honest person
would see me do this. Like I say, I'm good at doing this and I know
where to do it. The places that I do [my armed robberies] at, I don't
have to worry about a hardworking person passing by or a person
that pass by in a car, sees it, and calls the police. Where I do this
type of junk at, nothing but the dregs of society come through.
(No. 07)

Several of the offenders claimed that police officers often
refused to take drug robberies seriously; not only were the
victims of these offenses criminals, but they also were likely to
be hostile and uncooperative. As such, dope sellers or buyers

can be robbed with little fear of incurring legal sanctions, even if the incident should somehow come to the notice of authorities.

[The police] gonna [say] that, "Okay, this is a drug robbery. We really don't care about this [incident]. You shouldn't have been out selling this bullshit." You see what I'm saying? Like I said, yeah, I've thought about the risks of being caught, but . . . when you robbing drug dealers, it's a whole different agenda. (No. 07)

Obviously, robbing drug dealers and customers is not totally risk-free; there always is a possibility of violent retaliation (see, e.g., Oliver 1994). During our fieldwork, a number of robbers reported that they were being hunted down by one or more of their dope-dealing victims. In one case we experienced great difficulty convincing an offender to visit the scene of a recent drug robbery with us because he was afraid of being recognized and shot by the victims. When we picked him up for the visit, he was wearing dark glasses and a black sweatshirt with the hood pulled up tight. Even so, he insisted on riding in the back seat of our car, slumped down low. We arrived at the crime scene to find the crack dealers he and his partner had robbed two days earlier standing in front of a run-down liquor store. The offender reluctantly began to describe the stickup but quickly became frightened for his life and demanded that we leave as quickly as possible.

How [my partner and I] did this robbery, we put some ski masks on cause, you know, it's wintertime and people won't really identify [us]. But [the victims] still kind of knew who I was cause, man, they looking for me cause they knew my voice; they didn't see my face, but they knew my voice. . . . That's why I'm wearing these glasses and I'm wearing this hood and shit. I want to kind of cover myself up so they won't be shooting in this car. . . . Come on, let's get away from here, please. . . . I got to cut this [visit] off, man, I ain't fooling with you. They gonna end up killing me. . . . It's my life, man. I'm endangering you all's life [and] you all endangering my life too! (Red—No. 73)

We emerged from this incident unscathed. Several months later, though, the offender's crime partner was gunned down in the street. Rumor has it that the killing was the work of a dope dealer in retaliation for a stickup.

The likelihood that drug robbery victims will try to get even increases as one moves up the dope-dealing hierarchy. Recognizing this, most offenders in our sample did not attempt to rob persons who sold drugs in large quantities. Instead, they concentrated on street-level dealers, most of whom were young and had little status or influence in the drug underworld. These dealers typically lacked the organized network of intelligence and muscle necessary to exact retribution from those who robbed them. The offenders, almost to a person, viewed such dealers as punks who were prone to "fronting," that is, showing off and talking tough with little ability to back up their words.

[The street corner dope dealer is always] showing he's a punk. People like that are always fronting they stuff off. Every time they front they stuff off, they wonder why they getting jacked. . . . You never supposed to show what you got when you around me. (No. 25)

[These young drug dealers] walk around making it obvious that they have large sums of money; showing off very expensive jewelry. . . . They do everything wrong. [They're] big mouths, persons that tend to try to give the impression they are tough. . . . That's the easiest person [to rob]. (No. 04)

[The drug dealer] got all this money and shit and he won't fuck with us. I'm gonna rob him; see how he feels after I rob his ass. That's how I pick them people. I don't just rob any [drug dealer], I pick them kind of people on the set [who] think they all that. The ones that think they's the man. [He] ain't the man. I'm the man cause I'm gonna rob [him]. (No. 48)

Several offenders pointed out that some street corner dealers simply dismissed robberies as an occupational hazard and accepted their losses with equanimity. Often they were selling the drugs for someone else anyway and, if not, they could easily make up the shortfall by peddling more dope. As one said, "They don't have no choice, they got to accept it. It's all part of the [dope-dealing] game." Thus, the offenders reasoned, such dealers could be targeted with little concern that they would strenuously fight back or seek revenge.

A few of the offenders sometimes robbed major drug suppliers. Such robberies could be extremely lucrative, thereby eliminating the need to commit another stickup in the near future. But robbing high-level dope dealers is a hazardous undertaking. They seldom operate in the open and often surround themselves with protection; thus they typically are in a strong position to resist attempted robberies with deadly force. The trick, the offenders told us, is to catch these big-time drug suppliers "napping," that is, with their guard down. One offender, for instance, frequented several exclusive night spots popular among Saint Louis's black criminal fraternity in order to locate vulnerable dope dealers. Because he was a familiar figure in these establishments, he found it easy to gain introductions to out-of-town drug suppliers visiting the city on "business." He then enlisted an attractive female accomplice to lure these suppliers back to their hotel rooms with promises of sex. Once the intended victim had fallen asleep, the accomplice signaled to the masked offender, who stormed in, put a gun to the man's head, and demanded his money and drugs. The offender claimed that his victims invariably complied without protest: "What else they gonna do? I caught them with they pants down." A female armed robber who usually worked alone employed a similar strategy. She would cultivate relationships with high-level dealers in local nightclubs and take them to a nearby hotel. When the men undressed, she would put a knife under their testicles and threaten to "cut them off" if they did not hand over their cash.

Other offenders who sometimes targeted major drug suppliers did not rely on personal knowledge to select their victims but instead picked up inside information from sources on the street. These offenders did not have a formal arrangement for obtaining information, but their interest was well known on the street corner and people occasionally offered them tips about especially vulnerable targets. If the tip resulted in a successful score, the offender would share some part of the proceeds with the informant. Good tips, though, were infrequent. The secrecy inherent in the middle and upper echelons of the drug underworld meant that the vast majority of offenders had no realistic opportunity to rob major dope dealers. They did not run in the same social circles and lacked the criminal daring and the sophisticated interpersonal skills required to pull off such a crime.

While most of the offenders in our sample who usually chose criminal victims concentrated on drug dealers and customers, some of them preferred to rob other sorts of lawbreakers. Three, for example, typically targeted businessmen seeking the services of a prostitute. Two of these offenders—both women—were prostitutes themselves, while the third had a girlfriend who worked in the sex industry. From their perspective, the ideal robbery target was a married man in search of an illicit sexual adventure; he would be disinclined to make a police report for fear of exposing his own deviance.

[I pick a victim because] he looks married. He have a ring on. You kind of know when they are interested [in buying sex]. Some of them take [their wedding ring] off, but you can talk to them and find out [if they are married]. . . . They can't tell on us [for robbing them] because we do our little stuff. They stop us [on the street and] they buy us; that's why they don't report [the robbery]. (Nicole Simpson—No. 49)

Moreover, such a victim was likely to have a reasonable amount of cash on him, though this was not always the case.

Last night I went down to [a local entertainment district] and I wasn't looking to do nothing; I was just sitting [in a club] having fun. So this white guy came up to me and he said, "Would you like to party?" I said, "How much money you talking about?" He said, "I got as much as you want." I said, "No, it's not about that." He said, "What's your price?" I said, "Two hundred dollars." He said,

"Okay, let's go." We went downtown to his hotel. I said, "Do you want to take a shower?" And he went to take a shower, but he came out too quick. He tried to play on me; he wants sex for no money. He ain't got no money for real. So I had to do what I had to do, you know, cause he was trying to take advantage. When he had me on the bed, I just had my [pistol] on the side and put it to his head and did what I had to do. He didn't have no money. He didn't have no intention of paying nobody; he just wanted to get his thing off. But not with me! I done taken all of his stuff, his jewelry, his credit cards; he didn't have but ten dollars cash. He had checks and stuff like that, [but] he didn't have no cash on him. . . . that really pissed me off. (Jayzo—No. 22)

All three of these offenders had robbed both black and white men but preferred whites because they usually offered less resistance. As one said, "White guys be so paranoid [that] they just want to get away. . . . They not too much gonna argue with you." Likewise, each of them expressed a preference for intoxicated victims, who were viewed as good targets because they were in no condition to fight back.

Although these offenders had little difficulty identifying the characteristics of a perfect victim, it is important to remember that they were expressing preferences, not precise selection criteria. The very notion of deliberately selecting targets is inoperable where stickups evolve out of acts of prostitution. Asked about the way in which she picked her robbery victims, for instance, one of the prostitutes said, "I don't choose the victim, he chooses me." This may be over-simplifying the matter—after all, she did choose which of her customers to rob—but it is clear that, in these cases, the victims played an active part in the target selection process; the robberies emerged during an illicit encounter initiated by them in pursuit of their own criminal project.

The remaining offenders who specialized in robbing victims who were criminals reported targeting a hodgepodge of illicit street actors ranging from members of rival gangs to participants in neighborhood dice games. Their stickups had one thing in common; they flowed out of their other criminal involvements. Sometimes those involvements created the initial motivation to commit an armed robbery. In the following case, for example, an offender and several friends joined an illegal crap game with no intention of doing a stickup. But after sustaining heavy losses, they decided to get their money back.

We was invited by a friend of ours that used to live in our neighborhood to come over for a party, but the party was like a crap game. Everybody was shooting dice, and we lost a lot of money. There was a lot of money in this crap game. The dudes, we really didn't know these dudes, they was talking about [us losing all that money]. So when it was all over, all I knew was I wanted my money back, and the people who I was with was upset too. So they pulled out and I stayed, but I knew why I was staying. You know what I'm saying? So they came back with guns and everything. They had changed clothes, covered they faces and everything, pulled their hats down, and just robbed these guys. . . . When [my friends] came back, this one cat was trying to leave; he saw [the stickup] coming. . . . I was next to him and he saw them and he was trying to leave and I grabbed him and put a gun to his head. He upped his money. . . . [Then] we just slipped away. (Damon Jones—No. 34)

On other occasions, already motivated offenders seized an opportunity to commit an armed robbery that arose during an unrelated criminal pursuit, such as a gang fight. These offenders, faced with a pressing need for cash, had not set out objectively to find the best robbery target. They sought any quick and easy way out of their financial difficulties and thus were drawn to exploit the vulnerability of others in their immediate circle of criminal associates. This kind of behavior fuels the pervasive distrust of others that characterizes the social world of offenders (see, e.g., Anderson 1994). That distrust, in turn, often serves to justify the victimization of fellow criminals. As one armed robber told us, "It's a dog-eat-dog world. If I don't get them, they gonna get me." A vicious cycle develops in which high-crime neighborhoods inhabited by street offenders spiral into an ever-deepening chaos of predation and violence.

Noncriminal Victims

The threat of armed robbery makes a major contribution to the widespread "fear of crime that structures so much of everyday urban life" (Katz 1995:799). Many city dwellers consciously restrict their activities in an attempt to minimize their chances of being robbed. But little actually is known about how armed robbers select their noncriminal prey. Only when there is a better understanding of this process will lawabiding citizens have a realistic basis on which to judge their risk of being robbery victims and be able to take effective steps to reduce that vulnerability.

Thirty of the armed robbers in our sample routinely targeted law-abiding citizens. They did so at least in part because this was believed to be less dangerous than robbing other criminals. As one pointed out, "You don't want to pick somebody dangerous, they might have a gun themselves." Almost all of these offenders said that when faced with a pressing need for money, they usually first had to search for a suitable victim to attack.

I'm sitting at home [and] I got one cigarette left, no money. I'm thinking of ways to make some money. I may go down to the blood bank and give some blood, get ten dollars to get me a drink and some cigarettes with. [If] that don't work then I sit there and I think, "What can I do to try and get me some money?" I'll try and think of everything except the gun, [but] I know it's there all the time. Then I'll even think about, "Should I pawn the gun and then maybe when food stamps come out I could sell a few of my stamps to try and get this gun back? No, cause there ain't no telling when I might need it." Well, I can't think of nothing else [except armed robbery] . . . so I stick [the gun] in my pocket and I walk around and try to find an easy victim. (No. 71)

[I'm] broke. [I] don't have no money and no check come or something like that and [my paraplegic wife] be wanting to get high. . . . She just say, "You feel all right this morning?" I'll say, "Yeah, I feel okay." [And then she'll say], "You know, today is Wednesday, there ought to be some money down there now. You want to go down there and check it out? You up to it? We can get high." . . . I try to talk myself out of it, but . . . I know that once I open that door, it's all over; I'm gonna do [a stickup]. I'm gonna find somebody [to rob], you know. (Vick Smith—No. 75)

When searching for an armed robbery target, the offenders typically were required to make two basic decisions. First, they had to decide on a suitable area for their search. And second, they had to select a specific victim within this area. What factors underpinned their choices?

In selecting an area, the offenders did not have an infinite supply of places from which to choose. Both physical and psychological barriers limited their horizons (Brantingham and Brantingham 1981). Some offenders, for instance, did not have access to a car. This meant that, for all practical purposes, they were restricted to areas within walking distance (Lejeune 1977).

It's easier to go in the county [to do a stickup], but it's harder for us because we on feet. Nobody in my neighborhood has a car, unless they get they mother's or father's car, something like that. But we [can't] go burning up our mother's or father's car to go way out in the county to do a jack; we walk around the neighborhood looking for somebody [to rob]. (No. 56)

Even those with a car often were reluctant to journey far from their own neighborhoods because a long drive back might increase their vulnerability to apprehension.

I could tell you what would be my perfect area [in which to commit an armed robbery], but then I would not want to go out there because of the distance and the police and getting back to the city. The perfect area for me would be [an exclusive shopping mall on the outskirts of Saint Louis] because I know everybody that come through there got a lot of money . . . well-to-do white people. . . . But I've already did a [robbery] out there and got away with it so I don't want to keep chancing that one. . . . It would be hard to get back to the city. . . . Out in the county, out there, even if you are in a car, it's hard getting away because [the police] know to look for you on the highway. (No. 71)

Many offenders were dissuaded from traveling a great distance to commit their stickups by the immediacy of their need for cash. As one explained, "We just want to do [the armed robbery] and get it over with. We don't want to ride too far out of the way."

Beyond the practical constraints, there also were psychological factors that limited the range of areas available to the offenders. As Brantingham and Brantingham (1981: 37) have observed, a great deal of the territory that is objectively accessible to criminals is subjectively out of bounds, being "unknown . . . [and] populated with the terrors of the unfamiliar." Almost all of the offenders restricted their searches for potential robbery victims to locations with which they already were well acquainted. They knew the layout of the area and felt more comfortable or safer there (see also Feeney 1986).

You stay close to your home. You don't go too far past your boundaries because you don't know about everything. When you around where you live at you know more about it. You know when different people in, you know when the police is around. That's the best place to really stay. Just knowing your boundaries . . . because you got to get back home to feel safe. (No. 47)

[The Midtown neighborhood in the city] is the best area for me. It's my community and I know, say for instance if I had to run, I know every alley to get away. . . . out in the county [though], I would be lost. I could be up on [a busy business street near the Midtown neighborhood] and the police chasing me; I only stay six blocks from there. I know so many ways [to get away], I can go this way or that way and lose them. This is why I stay in the area [near where I live]. (Richard L. Brown—No. 82)

This typically meant staying within the jurisdictional boundaries of the city of Saint Louis and avoiding the more affluent environs of Saint Louis County, populated heavily by whites. Many offenders spoke of the county as if it were a land of forbidden fruits; a place chock full of tempting targets, but also one harboring great dangers for would-be lawbreakers. As they saw it, county residents were far more likely than their counterparts in the city to report suspicious behavior to the police.

> People in the city, I don't know what it is, but they are not too apt to call the police too often, and then a lot of them don't seem too concerned about what they see. They be like, "It ain't my business and don't make it yours cause you might get caught up in it." In the county [though], it's all totally different. (Burle—No. 80)

What is more, the offenders tended to steer clear of the county because the vast majority of its residents were white; they believed that, to avoid appearing suspicious, they had to blend in with the local population.

> I can go in a black neighborhood, [an] all-black neighborhood, and I don't stand out, as opposed to me going out there to [a shopping center in the county] where I might stand out. . . . I'm used to the streets of the city of Saint Louis. (Larry Washington—No. 19)

> [Suppose] you are running [away from a robbery] . . . you can't go in somebody's yard and try to hide [in the county]. Some black guy in somebody's yard out in [a well-to-do suburb in the county]? That doesn't work too good for me. (No. 71)

Finally, two armed robbers said that they did not commit offenses in the county because, among other things, the courts there were too punitive.

> I go everywhere [to commit my stickups] except for the county. . . . [The city jail] is like a penitentiary. [The county jail] ain't nothing for real, but [convicts] spend more time [there] than I would in the city. [Convicted armed robbers] will spend more time [in jail] out there than I would [in the city]. (No. 44)

> I have done some [armed robberies] in the county . . . and I will never commit that kind of crime [there] again. You get twice as much time in the county jail as you do in the city of Saint Louis. (No. 80)

It is arguable whether the offenders' perceptions of the county were accurate. But the important point is that, for a variety of reasons, most of them regarded sites beyond the borders of Saint Louis City to be off limits.

Target selection in street robbery differs from that in crimes such as residential burglary because potential victims are not anchored to any particular spot; they move from one place to another while going about their daily lives. This allowed some of the more enterprising offenders to target county residents without leaving the perceived safety of the city. They did this by searching for victims in and around the city's sporting venues and entertainment districts—areas known to attract a large number of visitors from the county. By targeting these areas, the offenders had the best of both worlds; they could remain in familiar territory while exploiting the riches of the hinterlands.

[Usually] I just start cruising and try to go to an area, gaming events, sporting events where people are going . . . where you assume [they] are going to take money. . . . they gonna buy tickets, have refreshments, you know. (No. 08)

Okay, like they got the Landing now, all that [area has] been redone up to that little highway part. Get up under that and you got the [gambling and river tour] boats, you got people walking back and forth, and then you got the other side over here [where] they got different clubs. . . . They got a lot of exotic clubs where [visitors] go congregate to drink and they be packed with money. . . . You can tell people who is coming in with money [and] you can tell when people don't. [The Landing] has that parking lot, well, anybody that want to [pull off a robbery], they can get that off there. (No. 74)

Such areas were regarded as especially good hunting grounds because they were easily reached from the offenders' own inner-city neighborhoods and they catered to a reasonably well-heeled clientele, many of whom were careless about their personal safety.

[I choose areas] where most of the people that come in there got money, that's plain and simple. . . . In Saint Louis [the perfect area

is an upscale entertainment district on the western edge of the city]
because [visitors] think they so protected down there. They got
police riding through there and most of the places got security
guards. But see, [visitors] leave themselves open because [they] let
they guard down. (No. 76)

Though virtually all of the armed robbers searching for
noncriminal victims were drawn to areas that they believed
were frequented by people who carried plenty of cash, there
was some disagreement about which places offered the most
lucrative targets. A number of the offenders reported that
they typically went straight to downtown Saint Louis to look
for potential victims because the offices and businesses located there tended to attract well-off people. As one put it,
"People [who] come downtown—the job, the white collar,
the suits, all those office buildings and shit—you [just] feel
that's where the money's at." Others preferred to search for
robbery targets in the city's poor, black neighborhoods, believing that the residents of such neighborhoods were more
likely to carry cash than the generally more affluent citizens
to be found downtown. Indeed, one offender became indig-
nant when we described the rundown section of the city in
which he committed his stickups as being poor: "People in
the ghetto got lots of money. The ghetto ain't poor. [The
people] there got more money on them than the people downtown. All they got is plastic and checks."

Within any given area, the armed robbers had clear ideas
about the best spots to find targets. These were microlevel
preferences, usually involving locations devoted specifically
to some sort of cash-intensive activity. The most popular sites
were around places to cash checks or automatic teller machines (see also Merry 1981).

[I've done] a lot of [stickups] at check-cashing places, especially
around the first of the month when food stamps and AFDC checks
come out because hundreds of people going in and out of there and
a lot of them are walking and you can catch one of them walking
down the street. You jump out of the alley on them. Most of the

time [when I want to find a robbery target] it's a place where people frequent a lot for money. (No. 19)

[I usually find potential victims at] check-cashing places, people go in there and cash their checks. Some people be walking to their cars [afterward]. You can walk right behind them. They come out of the check-cashing place and they get in they car and you stick the pistol right through the window and take the money. What can they say? What can they do? [Or] you got some people that cash a check and walking down the street and you just walk up behind them like you walking and just stick the pistol up under they arm. . . . You seen where they put the money at [and] you know what they got. (No. 47)

See, I know the places to go [to locate good robbery targets]. Usually I go to all the places where dope men hang out . . . but I [also have] done some people coming out of those instant tellers. . . . I'll go up to the car and they probably only getting like ten or fifteen dollars, but I'll make them get all of it. I'll say, "Give me all what's in that bank." [The victim is] probably gonna give me all of it. That's the perfect place . . . to [rob] a person. Them instant tellers, I love that! (No. 48)

These locations were followed closely in popularity by shopping mall and supermarket parking lots.

[When I want to find a promising target, I go] to large places of business like [a major downtown shopping center] or [to one of several supermarkets in the city] where I know there is a lot of people and where I know there will be money. . . . I'll spot somebody and then I'll follow them away to a less crowded area. (No. 71)

[As I said earlier, I like searching for victims around the city's entertainment districts. But] sometimes that gets burnt up. . . . Then I have to start spreading things around. . . . Grocery stores, that's the [next] best place, especially [during] this season, everybody [there] got some money. Ain't nobody walking up to [any of the local supermarkets] without no duckies. (No. 74)

In deciding where to offend, then, the armed robbers were influenced strongly by the potential reward; they wanted to find a location with an abundant supply of lucrative targets. The prevailing risk of detection also played a part in their location decisions. Many of them noted that the availability of good escape routes was an important criterion in selecting a robbery site. For those in cars, this usually meant choosing some place close to a major thoroughfare.

[To do a stickup I want] a place that is close to a freeway, close to a highway cause you definitely want to get away quick. (No. 08)

[For me to do a robbery someplace it] would have to be . . . by the park, like across from the park, see, that's a quick getaway. By the highway, the park and the highway; that would be my clean getaway if I had a car [at the time]. (Little Bill—No. 21)

Conversely, those on foot typically preferred to do their stickups where the escape routes were unsuited to automobile traffic. They saw this as increasing their chances of getting away should police officers attempt to chase them in a car.

[Doing stickups in areas with a number of restricted-access parking lots is good] because you can run across them, you can get away. Most of them, the way they made now, the police have to ride all the way up in there to come through the parking lot. All you got to do is jump over them steel things and keep running. By the time [the police officer] come all the way round and come up through the parking lot, you can come up in the next parking lot. Cause when [the officer] come out of that parking lot, it's an alley and [then] there is another parking lot and [the officer] got a steel barrier there, so he got to race down the alley to come back up the street. . . . All you got to do is jump [the barrier] because none of them that high, but [the officer] can't run his car over them. (No. 75)

One offender went a step further, telling us that he almost always committed his stickups within running distance of large public housing projects to thwart police officers who might be tempted to leave their automobiles and pursue him on foot: "They won't come up in [those places], and you got a lot of ins and outs. Police ain't used to that. I grew up in that type of area and [if] the police [were] chasing me up in one of them buildings, I'd lose them instantly."

A majority of the offenders in our sample also took into account the risk of being seen by passersby when choosing robbery locations. In an attempt to minimize this risk, most of them elected to commit stickups at night in poorly lit areas.

The perfect area [to commit an armed robbery] is at nighttime; city, county, it don't matter, nighttime. When it starts to get dark, that's the perfect time. (CMW—No. 17)

Even those who offended during the day typically favored areas in which shadows obscured the view.

[The best place to do stickups is downtown because] there are a lot of big companies down in there, skyscrapers. . . . It's always kind of dark down there for real [because] they got all them big buildings. (No. 75)

The two offenders in our sample who preferred to search for potential victims indoors displayed a similar concern to reduce the risk of being seen; both sought targets in restrooms at nightclubs, lounges, and bars because such places were not conducive to casual surveillance.

Surprisingly, only a handful of the offenders mentioned the level of police or security patrols as being worthy of serious consideration when choosing robbery locations. One said that he wanted to commit his stickups "a long way from any police station." Another noted that he tried to keep the police off balance by never offending in the same vicinity twice in a row. Yet another claimed that the best time to commit an armed robbery was when the police changed shifts, leaving the streets virtually unpatrolled for a short period. And a couple of offenders reported that it was important to time the movements of police and security guards so as to be able to avoid them. Therein lies the problem with police and security patrols as robbery deterrents; stickups often can be completed in a matter of seconds, and patrols cannot be everywhere at once. Indeed, during our earlier study of residential burglars we encountered an offender who switched to armed robbery whenever the police stepped up surveillance activities because stickups were faster and could be conducted in the open, where approaching patrol cars could easily be spotted.

In short, the armed robbers in our sample typically adopted a pragmatic approach when assessing the risks of potential robbery sites (see also Murray 1983). Did they stand a good chance of getting away? Were they likely to be seen by passersby? If the answers to those questions were yes and no respectively, most of them appeared to spend little extra time worrying about less predictable and more remote hazards (e.g., being surprised by a security patrol). Given that the offenders were desperate to get cash as quickly as possible, this makes perfect sense. From their perspective, it was better to get on with the offense than to ponder the risks indecisively.

Having settled on an area, the offenders next needed to locate a specific victim. They had to find an individual who was acceptable to them in terms of probable reward and potential risk (Lejeune 1977). This was a crucial decision. If the person they picked turned out to have little cash, they could not immediately move on to someone else for fear that the first victim might have called the police with a description of them. Worse yet, if they selected a target with the ability and determination to fight back, they could end up dead, seriously injured, or facing a murder charge.

A majority of the offenders were concerned first and foremost to locate an individual who was carrying a substantial amount of money. As one asked rhetorically, "If I'm gonna take the chance [anyway], why not take the chance for as much as I can get so I don't have to do this [again] anytime soon?" Typically they relied on outward signs to judge how much cash people were likely to have on them, including clothing, jewelry, and demeanor.

I'm a pretty good judge of character. I ain't come up empty-handed yet. . . . My wife kids me about that: "How'd you know they got money?" . . . [I know by] the way they dress and the way they act. They be dressed nice. Got on nice clothes, brand new clothes, and stuff like that. A lot of them act nervous and be walking real fast. . . .

Mainly people that got something you can tell cause they be looking behind them and all that, walking fast trying to get to they car.
(No. 75)

Most of the time you can tell [whether people have money] by
they clothes, the kind of jewelry they have on. (Bounty Hunter—
No. 35)

[Whether or not I decide to rob a particular person] depends on
what they got; like if they are wearing nice clothes, jewelry, and
you know, that's basically it. You can look at a person and just tell
if they've got money. . . . Sometimes people just walk around and
they tell everybody, "I got this much money and I got this [other
stuff]." (Lisa Jones—No. 40)

A number of offenders, all blacks, added that they also used
race to help them predict the amount of money in a person's
pocket. But there was no consensus as to whether whites or
blacks were more lucrative targets.

[Whites] got it all. They do. Man, look down on that Landing. . . .
young kids, young white kids, they just throwing money like, man,
look, I can't even do it now, and I'm forty-seven. I ain't just straight
up racial prejudiced or nothing, but I mean white folks just got the
money. Let's face it, they got the money. (No. 14)

Blacks, I don't know, it's like the first of the month [now] and the
majority of them are on welfare and that [money is] right there.
You can get the check or anything. . . . whites, they have credit
cards and checkbooks on them. They can cancel it off though; they
get robbed, they cancel it. So we rather get blacks. (No. 17)

[Whites] ain't got nothing I want. . . . I'm looking for jewelry,
money, nigger stuff. Most white people have about two dollars on
them and credit cards, something like that. (No. 44)

Judging the probable payoff in street robbery is far more
difficult than it is in, say, residential burglary. Whereas virtually all dwellings contain a fairly predictable range of valuable electronic goods (e.g., TVs, VCRs), people vary widely in
the amount of cash they carry. Outward appearance provided
the armed robbers with no more than a crude indication of

how much money potential victims were likely to have on them. As the two offenders quoted below remind us, appearances can be misleading.

A person dressed like a bum could have fifty thousand dollars in his pocket and this other guy, he dressed real sharp and very conservative looking, he ain't got fifty dollars in his pocket. So it's all just a chance in the dark when you . . . grabbing people on the streets. (No. 14)

[Judging how much money potential victims have on them is] weird because sometimes the ones you think have [a lot of] it won't have nothing but six or seven dollars in they pockets, and [sometimes] you see somebody that look like they got some money and all they got is jewelry. (No. 76)

Recognizing this, several of the armed robbers attempted to make more certain that the people they targeted were carrying plenty of cash. Those who typically stationed themselves near check-cashing places were in a particularly good position to do this; they easily could observe money being flashed in full view of everyone present.

[To find my robbery victims,] I would go out on [a local street] to one of those places they cash checks at. I don't hang out there [otherwise]. You just go out there and hang around. You just feel it out. . . . You can [soon] see the right opportunity. . . . You see a woman go in there and transact some business and she comes out of there with a big bag of money for a business . . . she gonna get [robbed]. (No. 47)

The sight of a person cashing a large check sometimes was enough to convince even unmotivated offenders that this was too good an opportunity to pass up.

[My most recent armed robbery victim] was a girl that had one of them support, alimony checks or something like that. I seen her cash it at a check-cashing place. I walked up on that; my mind wasn't on robbery, but like you say, I had about fifteen or twenty dollars in my pocket and I seen she had a big roll of cash. . . . I wasn't there to do a robbery, I was there waiting on a dude that owed me a hundred dollars. He was gonna cash a welfare check or SSI or some old check like that. I was waiting for him to give me my hundred dollars and then I seen this here. I saw this was [an] easy [way] to pick up four hundred dollars. (No. 02)

Signs of wealth, however, were insufficient in themselves to cause the offenders to single out individuals as robbery victims. Potential victims also had to be assessed as being low-risk. The offenders were unwilling to do a stickup, no matter how much money the intended victim appeared to have, when they perceived the chances of getting caught, injured, or killed to be too high. They wanted victims who they thought would hand over their cash without making a fuss; overcoming resistance could be dangerous and time consuming and could increase the chances of being caught in the act (see also Shover 1996).

In attempting to choose compliant victims, the armed robbers focused primarily on three factors that, they believed, were predictive of a person's inclination to resist attack. The first was race. Many of the offenders reported that, other things being equal, they preferred to rob whites because, compared to their black counterparts, such victims were more likely to be cooperative.

I've found a few blacks try to retaliate a little bit . . . if you offer them the opportunity, more so than whites. Whites accept the fact that they've been robbed. . . . But I've noticed that some blacks would rather die than give you they bucks and you damn near have to be killing [them] to get it. (Joe Thomas—No. 62)

[Whites] usually don't resist. A black person will try to grab the gun out of your hand. They will make you shoot them if you have to. . . . Black people say, "I don't care if you do have a gun," and they'll put up a hassle, whereas a white person might say, "Look here, take the watch, take this here, just don't hurt me.". . . A black person will say, "No, you got to kill me. You ain't gonna take my money like that." (No. 71)

If [the victim is] black they gonna try to get wrestling and it's gonna be too much trouble to try and take [the cash] from them. . . . [Whites] can get [the money] back easier [so they seldom resist]. . . .

Blacks hard to come by [cash] so they ain't gonna come up off it too easy. (No. 75)

Some of these offenders relied on white stereotypes of black criminals to intimidate their victims into compliance.

I rob mostly whites . . . that's where you get your money. I usually don't have no problem [with resistance], none at all. [Whites] got this stereotype, this myth, that a black person with a gun or a knife is like Idi Amin or Hussein. And [a] person [who believes] that will do anything [you say]. (James Williams—No. 06)

Even offenders who expressed a marked preference for white victims, however, often ended up robbing blacks instead. More than anything, this probably reflects the strongly intraracial character of social interaction in Saint Louis. Since most of these offenders perceived themselves to be under pressure to act quickly, they were primed to exploit the first opportunity that presented itself. When the chips are down, one offender reminded us, armed robbery "ain't about black or white, it's about green."

Sex was the second demographic factor used by the offenders to gauge the likelihood of victim compliance. Many of them claimed that women generally made better victims than did men because they were less inclined to fight back.

[Women are] easy; they very vulnerable, they so easy [because] they panic so quick. . . . women will throw they purse to you and you just snatch it or just tell them to give it up [and] they'll give it up without resisting. But men, they will hesitate sometimes [so that] you got to show them you are serious . . . shoot them in the leg or smack them with the gun. (No. 81)

See, women, they won't really do nothing. They say, "Oh, oh, okay, here, take this." A dude, he might try to put up a fight, and that would give you a reason to shoot him. (No. 17)

However, one offender was emphatic that, contrary to popular belief, women actually were riskier targets than were men.

He asserted that they had a tendency to panic and become hysterical, thereby attracting unwelcome attention.

I've seen a lot of women get hysterical [when someone pulls a gun on them]. A lot of men, they stay calm and they'll just give you their wallet. But a lot of women, they'll panic and they'll go hollering and screaming and you try to talk them into just shutting up and just being quiet, "Give me your purse." But they not really hearing what you saying because they get hysterical, you know? (No. 19)

The third demographic factor that the armed robbers took into account when trying to locate cooperative victims is age. Quite a few of the offenders expressed a strong preference for elderly victims because they were unlikely to offer any resistance.

[When I need to find a robbery victim, I look for an old person], maybe somebody up in they seventies . . . because you don't have to worry about struggling with them and being real forceful with them. They might just give [the money] to you anyway, to keep from being hurt I guess. (No. 83)

[I like to rob people in their] sixties and whatever. They gonna do what you say cause they afraid of getting hurt. They are timid people. (Loco—No. 38)

I usually try to get [my victims] as old as possible cause they the ones that gonna put up less fight; that's true. I pass up a lot of [people in their] thirties and get up to some fifties and some sixties. (No. 14)

The perfect kind of person to rob [is] an elderly person. I would say the easiest person, the perfect person, is the elderly white lady . . . cause nine times out of ten . . . they looking nervous . . . already scared that somebody gonna rob and hurt [them]. It's easy. All you got to do, like I said, [is say], "This is a robbery, don't make it a murder." [They will hand over the money quickly]: "Lord, here it is, I don't want to get hurt." (No. 82)

Beyond demographic indicators, a number of the offenders mentioned that they relied on subjective judgments about a person's current state of mental alertness. Several said that they usually chose victims who appeared to be intoxicated because, as one put it, "Drunks never know what hit them." Others reported that they typically targeted people who seemed to be oblivious to their surroundings, saying that such individuals were especially vulnerable to surprise attack.

[I prefer to rob] somebody that really ain't got they mind on what they doing. You can kind of feel people [and just know that] they ain't thinking about it: "I ain't worried about nothing, I ain't gonna get robbed." . . . That's the one that you get right there cause they ain't gonna be worrying about it. . . . They not paying attention. (No. 66)

For all of their talk about violence, few of the armed robbers relished the prospect of a fight; most of them tried hard to select victims who were unlikely to offer any resistance. This is not to imply that the offenders were incapable of looking after themselves. Some of them had been physically combative all of their lives and had earned fearsome street reputations for toughness. Rather, it underscores their strong desire to complete the offenses as quickly as possible so they can resolve their money problems and get back to partying. There is nothing to be gained and potentially much to be lost by having to struggle with a resistant victim.

In summary, the offenders who specialized in robbing noncriminal victims seldom traveled far in search of prey. For both practical and psychological reasons, most of them wanted to stay within the confines of Saint Louis City, their home turf. Even though the offenders typically were under pressure to act fast, they did not choose their targets randomly. Instead, they relied on their personal knowledge and beliefs about suitable robbery sites as well as on their perceived ability to read the signs indicative of the probable rewards and potential risks attached to robbing a specific individual. By no means, however, did the offenders attempt to locate the best robbery target objectively available to them. Far from it. In a state of financial desperation, they usually settled on the first person who appeared to meet their minimal subjective criteria for an acceptable victim.

COMMERCIAL ROBBERY

Armed robberies directed at commercial targets have consequences that extend well beyond the businesses victimized. To protect themselves against such crimes, businesses often adopt expensive security measures and pass the costs on to their customers. This puts businesses located in high-crime neighborhoods in a no-win situation because their clientele frequently are too poor to bear increased prices to support crime prevention measures (Reiss 1986). If the businesses do not provide extra security, however, their customers may feel unsafe and go elsewhere. Either way, the businesses suffer. And when these businesses fail or are forced to relocate in the face of an eroding customer base, the quality of life is reduced for the whole community. This quandary has been identified as one of the social calamities that can send urban neighborhoods spiraling into decline (Skogan 1986). Accordingly, it is important to develop a clear understanding of why and how active armed robbers choose commercial targets. Without this information, there is a danger that urban businesses will devote resources to costly crime prevention measures that have little effect on offender decision making.

Ten of the armed robbers we interviewed reported that they usually targeted commercial establishments; another three said that about half of their stickups were committed against such establishments. These offenders claimed that they liked robbing commercial targets because they could count on the ready availability of a reasonable amount of cash, something that could not be taken for granted with most street robberies.

[I prefer to rob a] business. Street robbery, it's all right, but unless you already know this type of person is carrying this type of money [it might not be profitable]. But these stores or something like that, you kind of know. . . . Money is going out [in the store], you know it's there. But you damn near guessing if this person [on the street] is gonna have it. You don't know. (No. 12)

Street robberies, usually there is a lot of unknown factors there. Just running up on people . . . *maybe* you got some information as to how much money that they carry, but one thing for sure, when you go into a commercial place they have a certain amount of money at any given time. This man [on the street] could be broke. But if you go in a convenience store, you gonna get some money. [Commercial robberies] pay off better. (Robert Jones—No. 11)

Large amounts of cash, in turn, extended the time between armed robberies and thereby reduced the offenders' overall exposure to the various risks inherent in the offense. As one told us, "I don't really do that many [commercial stickups] because, when I do, I get cash. It lasts for a while, you know."

A majority of the offenders who specialized in robbing commercial targets were low-level hustlers driven by immediate financial pressures to exploit close-at-hand opportunities. Liquor stores, taverns, and pawnshops were especially popular targets. By their nature, such places had to keep a considerable sum of money on the premises.

[The perfect robbery target is] a convenience store that sells liquor, cashes checks and sells liquor. [Those places have] a lot of money. (No. 11)

Me myself, I generally start off with places that's handling money. . . . You got a lot of taverns that cash checks might have seven or eight thousand dollars around at any given time. . . . Or [I might pick] a pawnshop, somewhere where, you know, they got seven, eight, or nine thousand dollars around. . . . I start off in that range there, somewhere where it would be worth my while to try to rob it. (No. 69)

Gas stations also were popular venues for stickups.

[The best robbery target is] a filling station, a small place. . . . It's a lot of those that are privately owned and are small so you can rob those pretty good. (Lavon Carter—No. 68)

The offenders, a number of whom worked alone, were drawn to these establishments because they typically were one- or two-person operations. But even two employees could present unacceptable risks to a lone robber, unless they were stationed close to one another.

Mainly I count on two [employees], no more than two. When there is two people, you try to get them both together. You can't have one over [on one side of the building] and one over [on the other side]. You have to mainly have them both together. (No. 68)

The offenders also were attracted to small businesses because, at any given time, such places seldom had more than a few customers. Customers were perceived as risky because they were hard to watch and their actions impossible to predict. One armed robber, for example, used to target supermarkets but now finds them too crowded for comfort:

I have robbed supermarkets before. Matter of fact, that is one of the things that I was convicted for. I used to rob supermarkets, but I've had difficulties in supermarkets because of the number of people that are involved. That's another thing that I'm looking for when I'm robbing, I'm trying to eliminate the amount of people that I'm dealing with. I want to kind of minimize that as much as possible. . . . I never would try to rob the whole supermarket, I would go to the booth where you cash your checks and that's what I would rob. I've always had difficulties. Used to have to take the security guard and put the pistol on him and walk him to the booth. You got people all around. Some of them don't know what's going on, some of them might. It's a lot more risky. (No. 69)

None of the commercial robbers who operated in and around their own high-crime neighborhoods expressed undue concern about security cameras. One said that he did not worry about such devices because "a lot of them will have monitors and not cameras; the monitors just hold the picture while you are there." Most robbers reported that it simply did not matter whether their pictures were taken; a pair of dark glasses, a baseball cap, or a ski mask could easily disguise their identity.

A lot of times I wear glasses. I wear dark glasses and I have a hat down and I just go in. (No. 68)

[Cameras] don't bother [robbers] cause we got ski masks on. . . . They can't get our faces [from those pictures]. (No. 16)

You can't go in no store [to commit a stickup] unless you wear a ski mask. I have one that you can pull into a skull cap that you can just roll up. (No. 12)

Security cameras, it seemed to us, had become so much a part of the urban commercial landscape that the armed robbers had begun to take their presence for granted and to plan accordingly; not once did we hear of an offender rejecting an otherwise desirable target because it had a camera.

The commercial armed robbers in our sample disagreed about the deterrence value of security guards. Some said that they would not attempt to rob an establishment while a security guard was on duty.

If [a store has] a security guard, then we just come back later. If that security guard still there, we just go to another store. (No. 16)

Others, however, reported that security guards were not much of a threat. This was especially true for offenders who committed their commercial stickups as part of a team.

There are a couple of guys that I work with. It's always at least three [of us] when we do those [commercial] robberies. We never go alone. For security you always have someone watch the floor . . . and [some]one might watch the security guard and take his stuff. That's really just a waste, a security guard being in there, unless he gonna just watch somebody steal something and pull out a gun and arrest them. That might stop a shoplifting or something. But as far as a security guard preventing a robbery, that's just a waste of money. And that's what they got him there for! [Preventing stickups is] what the security guard is there for. (No. 05)

One offender claimed that he and his partners used to target businesses with security guards purposely in the belief that this was a reliable indicator of the potential payoff.

> Most places [around us] got security guards. . . . For a while there, we wouldn't rob any[place] unless they had a security guard. That tell you they got money in there. So the first move would be, we would take turns, the first guy that's his job to go and disarm the security guard. (No. 69)

While the commercial armed robbers clearly considered prevailing risks and rewards when selecting their targets, there is a danger of reading too much rationality or professionalism into their decision making. Most of them chose targets in much the same way that street robbers selected likely victims. Faced with a pressing need for cash to continue partying, they robbed the first place that seemed reasonably safe and profitable; they displayed little inclination to search for the optimal target.

Street-based research is unlikely to tap into networks of highly professional criminals who, by definition, take great pains to minimize their risks while maximizing their profits. On the street, the vast majority of such offenders have a desire to remain anonymous that transcends whatever potential rewards might accompany participation in a social science research project. A prison-based study may yield more information about high-level armed robbers because, once inside, such robbers have less to lose by cooperating with researchers.

That said, our backup fieldworker did introduce us to three male friends who carried out commercial stickups in a careful, calculating manner. These offenders, who often worked together, traveled significant distances to rob jewelry stores in small towns throughout the midwest. In their eyes, small-town jewelry stores were perfect targets; they typically contained plenty of valuable merchandise but lacked the sophisticated security systems associated with big-city jewelers. Even the police in small towns were perceived as being less vigilant and capable than their metropolitan counterparts. As one of the offenders put it, "I ain't gonna say they dumb. They just behind the times."

These offenders did not choose their own targets. Instead, they relied on the services of a professional fence who told them where and when to commit their stickups, specified exactly what jewelry was to be taken, and disposed of the stolen merchandise afterward.

Whenever the dude comes up with something, he calls me. Tell me to get in touch with everybody. . . . Believe me, I do not know [how the fence chooses the jewelry stores]. All I know is that me and him, like I said, small towns is the thing. How he goes about planning, how he goes about finding it, it's all in his head. Only thing we know is what we got to do when it's that time. . . . [The fence tells us] where is the place at, what we got to get out of the place, and what we got to do when we get back [to Saint Louis]. (Nick—No. 72)

As a result, these robbers had little control over the timing of their stickups and thus had a strong incentive to budget their money. Like their less professional peers, however, they were so caught up in desperate partying—one gambled heavily, and all three were addicted to heroin—that it was difficult for them to control their spending. Each admitted that he sometimes was forced to commit a more impulsive armed robbery to tide himself over until the next big offense.

SUMMARY

When confronted with an immediate need for cash, the vast majority of offenders in our sample do not venture far in their search for suitable victims. In fact, most of them typically prey on other local criminals, especially street corner drug dealers. Drug dealers are good victims because they carry plenty of cash and are in no position to make a police report. The possibility that some robbers might serve a useful function by helping to restrain neighborhood drug markets has largely been overlooked by previous researchers, at least in part because they based their conclusions on interviews with incarcerated offenders. Criminals who specialize in robbing drug dealers are unlikely to be found behind bars.

Not all of the offenders we interviewed target criminal victims. A substantial number usually rob law-abiding citizens. In picking their victims, these offenders are primarily concerned with making sure that the person selected has ready cash. They attempt to do this by relying on easily observed cues such as dress and demeanor. The offenders also are anxious to choose victims who will hand over their money without protest. For this reason, many of them prefer to rob whites, who are widely regarded as less likely than blacks to offer resistance. This may go some way toward explaining why robbery, unlike other forms of criminal violence, frequently is an interracial offense involving a white victim and a black offender.

Our sample included only a small number of commercial armed robbers. Most of them were low-level offenders who, like the street robbers, searched for targets in and around their own neighborhoods. Prison-based research also has demonstrated that armed robbers typically do not travel far in search of targets. That research, however, failed to make clear the extent to which the self-indulgent activities promoted by street culture discourage extended searches. Desperate to obtain quick cash to keep the party going, most armed robbers are primed to settle for the first, rather than the best, target available to them. The cool rationality that characterizes the target-selection decisions described by imprisoned armed robbers is in short supply on the streets.

4 Committing the Offense

Having settled on a specific robbery target, the next job for offenders is to commit the stickup. This is a complex undertaking, involving a set of actions that have to be performed in the face of a "problematic outcome and potentially serious consequences" (Shover 1991:103). Not only must offenders compel inherently reluctant victims to comply with their demands, but they must do so under considerable emotional pressure in an environment fraught with potential hazards. How do they accomplish this feat? That is the question to which this chapter is devoted. This issue has important implications for our understanding of offender decision making. Such decision making does not end with the selection of a target. Indeed, the decision to commit a stickup itself is subject to reversal, at least in theory, up to the moment when the offender confronts the victim with a weapon. And once that has occurred, the offender must continue to make crucial decisions throughout the commission of the offense.

Unlike most sorts of crime, successful armed robberies are never secret or ambiguous. By definition, they require offenders to confront intended victims directly, letting them know in no uncertain terms that a stickup is in progress. As such, armed robberies invariably include a strong interactional component; offenders and victims must develop "a common definition of the situation" and co-orient their actions to meet the demands of the offense (Luckenbill 1981:25). This does not happen automatically. After all, why should stickup victims willingly participate in their own fleecing? Offenders typically must employ threatened or actual violence to induce cooperation. But to threaten violence is to set in motion an interactive chain of events in which neither party can know for sure what will happen next. Both offender and victim are trying desperately to predict the other's actions so they can launch a preemptive strike. In such a situation, the danger of a "fateful misreading" is omnipresent; any miscalculation could result in serious injury or death (Katz 1991: 285). Experienced armed robbers know this, and that awareness influences their actions at every stage of the offense.

THE ILLUSION OF IMPENDING DEATH

To be successful, armed robbers must take control of the offense from the start. They immediately have to impose on the interaction a definition favorable to their ends, allowing intended victims no room for negotiation. This typically is accomplished by creating an illusion of impending death.

Robbery itself is an illusion. That's what it's about. . . . Here is a person that you stick a gun in his face, they've never died, they don't know how it feels, but the illusion of death causes them to do what you want them to do. (No. 11)

A large part of creating such an illusion involves catching potential victims off guard; the element of surprise denies them the opportunity to adopt an oppositional stance.

Sometimes people be alert; they be watching so you got to be careful of what you do. You got to be alert. . . . Pretty soon [the intended victim] falls asleep, and then I got that nigger right then. . . . He ain't even tripping. He over there looking at some girl. . . . he probably just take his eyes off what he's doing, watching out, [which is] what he's supposed to be doing, and just turn his head on some girls. And [the stickup] be on. (No. 44)

Approaching the Target

The offenders in our sample employed two different methods to approach would-be victims without arousing their suspicion. The first method involved using stealth or speed to sneak up on unwitting prey (see also Luckenbill 1981).

You just walk up to [intended victims]. You creep up on them [and], when they turn they heads, you just hurry up and run up on them, put the gun to they head and tell them, "If you move, you dead. Freeze up!" (Swoop—No. 50)

[Whomever I am going to rob, I] just come up on you. You could be going to your car. If you are facing this way, I want to be on your blind side. If you are going this way, I want to be on that side where I can get up on you [without you noticing me] and grab you: "This is a robbery, motherfucker, don't make it no murder!" I kind of like shake you. That's my approach. (No. 82)

When using this method, most of the offenders preferred to approach victims from the rear to avoid being seen.

If I'm running up on them, [I approach victims] from the back and I got the strap on, or knife, or whatever. I'll tell them: "Don't move! Just don't turn around. Don't look me in the face." . . . And if [they] attempts to turn around, I let them know. I done had to stab a couple of people, but I ain't never had to shoot nobody. (No. 31)

[If the victim is] walking down the street, then just go right behind them [and] put the gun to her head and just start snatching her stuff. You say something like, "You look back, we gonna kill you!" Basically that's it; she all shaked up and everything. That's the best, get them from behind. (No. 17)

A few offenders, however, said that they usually confront victims head-on to show them that they mean business.

My usual way [of committing an armed robbery] is face up. . . . I rob a lot of people that deals with drugs. Getting behind them so they don't see your face, they buck you; they want to turn around and think you jiving. But a lot of them be high off drugs theyself, so I'm used to making them see the pistol, look at it and look at me

and make sure that they understand that I mean business, I'm for
real. . . . When you facing the back of [the victims'] head, you don't
know what they thinking and they don't know if you are playing or
not. . . . I look very serious at them, I'm staring right at them and I
let them know that I'm for real about it. This ain't no joke. Let him
know that if he don't do what I tell him, I'm gonna blow his face
off. (No. 01)

Either way, the intent is to lurk in the background and to
strike "out of nowhere," giving victims no advance warning
and little opportunity to take evasive action.

The second method used by the offenders to approach intended victims involved "managing a normal appearance"
(Luckenbill 1981:29). The aim was to fit into the social setting such that victims saw their presence as normal and nonthreatening, thereby allowing them to get close enough for a
surprise attack.

I rap with [drug dealers], shoot the breeze, chit-chat with them.
Might play box with them [to] see if they got a pistol on them or
whatever. . . . I might approach them and pretend like I want to buy
some dope from them. While they trying to go in they bags and
get me some dope or whatever, I'm gonna be like, "Give it all up!"
I tell them [to] brace theyself. (No. 63)

Most of the time . . . we just go up to [the victim], "What's up,
man? Do you know where so-and-so street is?" Soon as [the vic-
tim] turns around I'm gonna bust him, just hit him. (Cooper—
No. 24)

Well, if I'm walking, say you got something that I want, I might
come up there [and say], "Do you have the time?" or "Can I get a
light from you?" Something like that. "Yeah, it's three o'clock." By
then I'm up on you, getting what I want. (No. 38)

Dressing in a clean-cut manner was one popular strategy employed by offenders to camouflage their predatory
intentions.

You got to be just another person walking up the street, [so] I keep
myself fairly presentable so I don't look like I'm no direct threat
to [the would-be victim]. So a guy looks behind him and sees me

coming and he will just turn back around and I [will be] up on him before he knows it. That's how I would get him. (No. 07)

Another strategy employed by some of the armed robbers involved using a female accomplice to lull would-be victims into complacency. The offenders who specialized in robbing small-town jewelry stores, for example, occasionally used a woman friend to help create a nonthreatening image; she would enter intended targets on the arm of one of the robbers, pretending to be shopping for an engagement ring.

You just go in [to the store], you and your girl [and one of the two other offenders]. Just do what you got to do. . . . I'll tell my [supposed] girlfriend, "Look, I want to pick this ring out." We sitting up there, once we get the woman or the man onto the little floor things, pulling everything out [of the cases], putting everything on the counter, and [my girlfriend] says, "I like that one. I like that." I say, "I thought I was the one supposed to be giving this to you. . . . Don't be [interfering], let me pick out the ring. You just go . . . and stand over there somewhere." So she'll go over there and she standing at the big window like she's looking at something and waves to [the other robber, who is waiting in the car]. The dude is always gonna be parked to where she can wave him in. When he sees her, that means for him to come in. Now nine times out of ten I got most of the jewelry up on top of the counter, the stuff that's valuable. I'll tell [the shop assistant], "I don't want none of them fifteen-, sixteen-hundred-dollar rings cause I can't afford it." So [the shop assistant] will stand in like the three-hundred- or four-hundred-dollar section . . . but I already done peeped where the rest of them at. I say, "What's that?" [And the shop assistant will tell me], "Oh, that's fifteen hundred dollars there." I say, "Oh, no, what's that over there [cost]?" So I know exactly which is the expensive ones for sure. . . . From there on out whatever I see, "Let me check out that one down there." Once he bend down, I flash on him: "Okay, this is a robbery!" When he raise back up . . . I already know what type of person this is, if he is going to be a problem or is he just going to give it to me like a chump. So I pull my gun out, I flash it: "This is a robbery! Get over in that corner!" (No. 72)

Compared to their male counterparts, female armed robbers had a decided advantage in attempting to normalize their

appearance. Sex role stereotyping meant that they were unlikely to be seen as potential offenders in the first place. What
is more, the sort of men they encountered during their daily
rounds tended to view them as sex objects and thus often
were oblivious to their capacity for violence.

Some dudes try to talk to us and it's like, okay, they stupid, but we
go along with they little game. We get in the car, then ride with
them. They thinking we little freaks, excuse my language, whores
or something. So they try to take us to the motel or whatever [and]
we going for it. Then it's like they getting out of the car and then
all my [girl]friend has to do is just put the gun to his head. . . . He
really can't do nothing, his gun is probably in the car. (No. 17)

The women who worked as prostitutes were especially
well placed in this regard; the nature of their business made it
easy for them to get close to intended victims without arousing their suspicion. In a sense, their apparent willingness to
engage in one form of deviance served as a cover for deviance
of a much darker sort.

[The victim] be so eager [for sex], he just go in there and drop his
pants. So that give me the opportunity to do what I got to do. . . .
It's just easy, you know. He leaves himself open for that, in other
words. If [he] was more cautious . . . that wouldn't happen. . . . So I
get [him]. That's my purpose in being up there [in the hotel room],
to get him. And if I have to use force, I come prepared. I always got
my hand on my gun. I keep my hand on that at all times. (No. 22)

The method chosen to approach potential victims typically
was dictated more by situational factors than by the idiosyn-
cratic preferences of individual offenders. Depending on the
situation, most of the armed robbers were prepared to use either speed and stealth or the presentation of a nonthreatening self to move within striking range of their victims. The
offender quoted below, for example, reported that he and his
partners usually initiate their commercial stickups simply by
charging through the front door of the establishment, ski
masks pulled down and guns drawn.

When I approach the door [of a would-be commercial target], generally we got ski masks that rolls up into a skull cap; it's a skull cap right now and as we get to the door, right prior to walking in the door, we pull our masks down. Once we come in, we got these masks down [so] we got to come in pulling our weapons, might even have them out prior to going in, just concealed. As soon as we pull those masks down, we are committed [because our intention is obvious]. (No. 69)

He added, however, that circumstances occasionally require them to enter intended targets posing as customers instead. Doing so helps them to avoid tipping their hand too early, which is crucial in situations where the victim is likely to be armed.

Say for instance [the target is] a tavern and the guy behind the bar . . . might be the kind of guy that got a pistol. Most bartenders and most people that's cashing checks, they got pistols on them. Believe me, they got pistols. . . . So in that particular situation, you got to . . . get in the door before you go into motion because you got to know where they are at. You've got to make sure that you've got a real chance to get up on them and make it not worth their risk to try to reach the pistol [before you betray your intentions]. (No. 69)

Armed robbers who worked together sometimes incorporated both methods of approach into a single offense; one of them would adopt a nonthreatening persona to distract the victim, thereby making it easier for the other to use speed and stealth to launch a surprise attack. Here again, the distraction of choice often involved a female offender who relied on her charms to lure male victims into a position of vulnerability.

I usually work with my fiancée, robbing tricks, you know. . . . She gets them and they be vulnerable. She stands on the corner and she sees a trick. She flags him down; he pull over on his own. Once she finds out that he got a little money, then it goes like that. We have a motel already waiting . . . that's close around by the whores' stroll and it's in the neighborhood. We pay for it in advance, the room.

I'm waiting at the motel. She has to do her thing, she give me the signal, flip the light on and off like that . . . and then I'm in there. It's a robbery. . . . Once he got his pants down, you know, it's just easy. (No. 13)

If [the intended victim] is a dude . . . I just walk up, "Hey, what's up? My name is whatever." Just basically get to know [the intended victim] a little bit. We exchange numbers, get to know each other a little bit. [So] we be standing there, we be talking [and my accomplice] will come up from behind and . . . say, "I'm gonna do you!" I'll probably just run off and we'll just meet up somewhere. . . . That's how you do it, just like a hunter. If a hunter sees a deer, and the deer know the hunter watching, he gonna try to strategize where the hunter can't kill him. But that hunter got to think, "What can I do to get this deer?" (No. 31)

A few offenders who usually operated alone also combined both methods of approach to carry out their stickups, as in the following case, where a robber shadows his victims for a considerable distance pretending to be a fellow shopper before using speed and stealth to complete the offense.

Once I spot somebody [to rob], I won't let them know that I am paying any attention to them at all. I saw you in the store. I was looking at you [and thinking]: "Boy, that's a nice jacket you got on there." And then you reach in your pocket and pull out a wallet full of money. Nice ring, nice wallet, pocket full of money. . . . Then I'll follow them around and I'll go outside. Usually I'll go out before they come out. I'll stand there and I be watching them. I see them come out. I kind of walk away from the door. I watch how far they might have to go to get to their car. . . . I'll come up toward them, not behind them. Like if I see them coming to the car, I'll cut over and I'll come up the other way. If they go [the other] way, I'll cut over that way like I'm going to my car too. When I see them pull they keys out, I know they at the car and I'll come on up: "Open the door. Give me your money. Don't make no scene. I don't want to have to hurt you." (No. 71)

Regardless of the manner in which the offenders make their approach, the aim almost invariably is the same: to "establish co-presence" with the victim without tipping their hand (Luckenbill 1981:29). This gives would-be victims little opportunity to recognize the danger and to take steps to repel the attack. Not only is this far safer for the offenders, it also puts them in a strong position when it comes to generating the victim's immediate compliance. The offenders, it will be remembered, typically perceive themselves to be under pressure to get money quickly. Further, they do not want to linger for fear of being caught in the act. As a result, they are anxious to avoid becoming embroiled in time-consuming negotiations with their victims, seeking instead to scare them into a state of unquestioning cooperation by creating an illusion of impending death. This is accomplished much more easily when victims have not been given an opportunity to develop an alternative interpretation of the situation beforehand.

Announcing the Stickup

By announcing a stickup, armed robbers commit themselves irrevocably to the offense. Any semblance of normality has been shattered; from this point onward, the victim will act and react in the knowledge that a robbery is being committed. The offenders we interviewed saw this as the "make or break" moment. The challenge for them was "to dramatize with unarguable clarity that the situation ha[d] suddenly and irreversibly been transformed into a crime" (Katz 1988:176). In effecting this transformation, they were seeking to establish dominance over their intended prey, thereby placing themselves in a position to dictate the terms of the unfolding interaction.

When I first come up on [my victims], I might scare them, but then I calm them down. It's a control thing. If you can get a person to listen to you, you can get them to do just about anything. . . . That's the way the world is made. (No. 08)

Most of the offenders said that they typically open their armed robberies with a demand that the would-be victim stop and listen to them.

I say [to the victim], "Look here, hey, just hold up right where you at! Don't move! Don't say nothing!" (No. 14)

They often couple this demand with an unambiguous declaration of their predatory intentions.

[I tell my victims], "It's a robbery! Don't nobody move!" (No. 13)

That declaration, in turn, usually is backed by a warning about the dire consequences of failing to do as they instruct.

[I say to the victim], "This is a robbery, don't make it a murder! It's a *robbery*, don't make it a murder!" (No. 48)

All of the above pronouncements are intended to "soften up" victims; to inform them that they are about to be robbed and to convince them that they are not in a position to resist.

Having seized initial control of the interaction, offenders then must let victims know what is expected of them (Luckenbill 1981). As one armed robber reminded us: "You have to talk to victims to get them to cooperate. . . . They don't know what to do, whether to lay down, jump over the counter, dance, or whatever." This information typically is communicated to victims in the form of short, sharp orders laced with profanity and, often, racial epithets.

[I say to victims], "Hey, motherfucker, give me your shit! Move slow and take everything out of your pockets!" (James Love— No. 27)

I'll say something [to the victim] like, "Motherfucker . . . give me your money! All of it! Now!" (No. 77)

[I grab my victims and say], "Take it off, girl! Nigger, come up off of it!" (Libbie Jones—No. 57)

The "expressive economy" with which the offenders issue instructions can in part be accounted for by a desire to keep

victims off balance by demonstrating an ominous insensitiv-
ity to their precarious emotional state (see Katz 1988:177).
Clearly, the swearing and racial putdowns help to reinforce
this impression.

Beyond this, however, the offenders have several additional
reasons not to say too much to their victims. Foremost among
these is a concern that their voices might give them away.

> You don't say too much, man. . . . You don't want the victim to
> know your voice. (No. 44)

> A lot of people I get, I either know them or know them through
> someone [else]. I try not to say too much; they might know my
> voice. (No. 63)

Recall also that most of them are operating under intense
emotional pressure and are anxious to remove the perceived
cause of that pressure as quickly as possible. In such circumstances, extended conversation merely serves to increase risk
and delay gratification. And frankly, the vast majority of
armed robbers lack sophisticated communication skills and
see little point in talk; brute force is their preferred medium.

All but four of the eighty-three offenders who addressed
the issue of weapons reported that they typically used a gun
to announce their stickups. They recognized that displaying a
firearm usually obviated the need to do much talking. As one
said, "A gun kind of speaks for itself." Most of them believed
that "big, ugly guns" such as 9MMs or .45s were the best
weapons for inducing cooperation.

> [A .45], that's my gun of choice. . . . It's one of the most hard-
> hitting guns in the world and it's big enough to scare a person.
> You don't even have to have bullets in it; just the sight of it will
> put something on [the victim's] mind. (No. 07)

> The bigger gun has more of a tendency to intimidate the victim
> and lessen the chance of them trying to [resist]. (Larry Brooks—
> No. 20)

[The 9MM] got that look about it like it gonna kill you. It talk for itself: "I'm gonna kill you." Looking at a nine pointed at you, that's what goes through your head: "He gonna kill me if I don't give him this money." (Prauch—No. 84)

In practice, however, many of the armed robbers actually carried somewhat smaller firearms—snub-nosed .38s were especially popular—because they were more easily concealed and simpler to handle.

The best weapon is something small, something that is not heavy. . . . I know a bigger weapon will put more fear in a person, and if it comes to where it has to be used, I feel better with a big one. But I truly think that the best weapon is something small, a .38, something like that; it's not heavy [and] it will kill almost just as quick as something bigger. You can carry it and it's almost like you don't have anything; not a lot of excessive weight. (No. 04)

I like the .32 because it's like a .38, small, easy, and accessible. And it will knock [the victim] down if you have to use it. (No. 09)

A few offenders maintained that very small-caliber pistols (e.g., .22s, .25s) made poor robbery weapons because many potential victims were not afraid of them.

[With] .22s or .25s people gonna be like, "Man, he using this little gun. I ain't worried." . . . A .22 is real little, they gonna be, "Man, that ain't gonna do nothing but hurt me. Give me a little sting." (Syco—No. 67)

That said, the majority of respondents felt that even the smallest handguns were big enough to intimidate most people. One offender put it this way: "A person's gonna fear any kind of gun you put in their face. So it don't matter [what you use]. If it's a gun, it's gonna put fear in you."

The quandary faced by offenders in relying on a gun to induce fear is that the strategy might work too well. As Katz (1988) has observed, the display of a firearm can easily be misinterpreted by victims as the precursor to an offense far more serious than robbery (e.g., rape, kidnapping, murder). Offenders are keen to avoid such misinterpretations because they can stun victims into a state of incomprehension or, worse yet, convince them that determined resistance represents their only chance of survival. When armed offenders warn victims—"This is a robbery, don't make it a murder!"— they are doing more than issuing a credible death threat. Paradoxically, they also are seeking to reassure the victims that submission will not put their lives in jeopardy (see Luckenbill 1981).

In announcing their stickups, then, offenders are attempting to strike a precarious balance. They must threaten would-be victims sufficiently to compel compliance without either immobilizing or emboldening them through excessive fearsomeness. After all, victims who are unable or unwilling to cooperate can make it much more dangerous and difficult for offenders to effect the transfer of goods.

Transferring the Goods

No doubt the most difficult aspect of pulling off an armed robbery involves managing the transfer of goods. The difficulty lies in keeping the victim under strict control while, at the same time, making sure that everything worth taking has been confiscated. What is more, all of this must be accomplished as quickly as possible. The longer the stickup lasts, the more risk offenders run of being discovered by the police or passersby.

The armed robbers we interviewed used two different strategies to manage the transfer of goods. The first strategy, preferred by twenty-seven of the fifty-eight offenders who talked about this issue, involved simply ordering victims to hand over their possessions.

I let [the victims] give [their cash and valuables] to me. I ain't gonna touch nobody. If I got to search for it that's time limit, that's stalling. And I know about stalling. I'm trying to make [the offense] as quick as possible. They know where [the valuables are] at. We ain't gonna play no games. "Give it here!" (No. 74)

I tell [my victims], "Man, if you don't want to die, give me your money! If you want to survive, give me your money! I'm not bull-shitting!" So he will either go in his back pocket and give me the wallet or the woman will give me her purse. (No. 81)

By making victims responsible for the transfer of goods, the offenders were able to devote their undivided attention to watching for signs of danger.

I rather for [victims] to give [their valuables] to me because I have to be alert. If they reach for something, I'll have to shoot them. (No. 60)

I have [my commercial victims] put [the cash] into a bag . . . cause I can watch while they doing it. If I'm doing it, I have to look at the money and the bag while I'm putting it in there, and then watch the victim. (No. 79)

There is, however, one serious drawback to giving victims responsibility for the transfer; it is difficult to know whether they really have turned over all of their valuables. Recognizing this, many of the offenders employed tough talk and a fierce demeanor to discourage victims from attempting to shortchange them.

You never really know [if the victim is holding back], they may have some [valuables] stashed somewhere else. But hopefully when you tell them what you gonna do to them if they don't give you all of it, then hopefully that's when they give you all of it. (No. 06)

You say, "Is that everything?" You can kind of tell if they lying sometimes: "That's all I got, man, that's all!" You'll say, "You're lying, man, you lying!" and just make them think that you're get-ting pissed because he's lying to you. So basically you got this gun [pointed] at they head, so sometimes it be like, "Okay, I got some more." (No. 34)

You don't [know if the victim has deceived you]. You just basically hope that you put enough scare into them where they giving it [all]

to you. I have had that to happen; I have actually went on a robbery and found out that most of the money was left [behind].
Some guys just won't give it to you. You think you're getting it,
but they might have a secret hiding place you don't know about.
(No. 69)

Some of these offenders actually searched their victims—
albeit often summarily—to check whether they had given
them everything.

Sometimes I feel they pockets [afterward]. A lot of [victims] be lying and saying, "That's it." But they still have a lot of money.
(Menace—No. 36)

You take your little pat-down [before leaving]. You feel a wad, you
gonna go groping for it: "Empty that one!" And socks. The hell
with them shoes. If they got socks on, yeah, [I search the tops of
them]. But I'm not gonna wait for them to take they shoes off. I
ain't gonna do that. (No. 76)

A few went so far as to rough up their victims, especially
those who appeared confused or hesitant, to reinforce the
message that attempting to hold out on them would be a risky
proposition (see also Lejeune 1977; Katz 1988).

Well, if [the victim] hesitates like that, undecided, you get a little
aggressive and you push them. Let them know you mean business.
I might take [the] pistol and crack their head with it. "Come on
with that money and quit bullcrapping or else you gonna get into
some real trouble!" Normally when they see you mean that kind
of business they . . . come on out with it. (No. 80)

But most of the offenders who allowed victims to hand over
their own possessions simply accepted what was offered and
made good their escape. To get greedy, they argued, was to
court disaster. As one explained, "You just got to be like,
'Well, it's cool right here what I got.' When you get too
greedy, that's when [bad] stuff starts to happen."

The second strategy used by the armed robbers to accomplish the transfer of goods, favored by twenty-one of the

fifty-eight offenders who discussed the matter, involved taking the victim's possessions without waiting for what was offered (see also Luckenbill, 1981).

I go in [the victim's] pockets. I don't wait for nobody to give me nothing. (No. 44)

I get [the victim's money] because everybody not gonna give you all they got. They gonna find some kind of way to keep from giving it all. (No. 82)

A number of the offenders who preferred this strategy were reluctant to let victims empty their own pockets for fear that they were carrying a concealed weapon.

I don't let nobody give me nothing. Cause if you let somebody go in they pockets, they could pull out a gun, they could pull out anything. You make sure they are where you can see their hands at all times. (No. 24)

I take [the money] cause I don't want [my victims] going in they pockets. A lot of drug dealers keep small .25 calibers in they front pockets. I don't want to take no chance of them going in they pocket, getting that pistol out, and shooting. That's why I check they pockets [myself]. (No. 63)

Most of the time I like to go in [the victims'] pockets [myself] cause I don't know what they got in they pockets; they probably have a gun and everything. (No. 78)

To outsiders, these offenders may appear to be overestimating the risk of encountering an armed victim. Such a perspective, however, betrays a respectable, middle-class upbringing. In the desperate inner-city neighborhoods in which almost all of the armed robbers reside and in which many of them ply their trade, weapons are a ubiquitous feature of everyday life.

While prohibiting victims from assisting in the transfer of goods can prevent them from gaining access to a concealed weapon, this strategy carries hazards of its own. Offenders cannot effect such transfers at arm's length. They must move into close contact with the intended victim, thereby becoming vulnerable to counterattack. Nor can they devote their full attention to watching for warning signs of impending danger. They also have to locate and secure the victim's valuables. Thus it is not surprising that many of the offenders who operated in this manner preferred to work with others; accomplices could watch their backs, freeing them to concentrate on the task at hand.

You got [the victim] right there in a headlock and, like, I can be checking in the pockets while [my partner] has the gun up to [the victim's] head. (No. 17)

I grab [the victim's possessions] . . . I take everything [myself]. People got my back, I ain't worried about nothing. (K-Money #1— No. 43)

Accomplices also sometimes could help minimize the time and effort required to locate the victim's possessions. The best example of this was provided by the offender in our sample who usually teamed up with his prostitute girlfriend to rob her clients. This offender had a decided advantage when it came to determining where victims had stashed their cash and valuables; his partner could surreptitiously tip him off— "give him the eye"—even while she pretended to be a victim herself.

[I know where the victim keeps his money] cause my gal, she gonna tell me where it's at. She gonna give me the eye. . . . That's her job. . . . She might have some money laying on the dresser [and] I might take that [too]. (No. 31)

Ten of the armed robbers who described how they managed the transfer of goods could not specify a typical strategy. Some of these offenders claimed that whether or not they allowed victims to assist in this process depended on their assessment of the trustworthiness of the individual standing before them. Although objective characteristics such as the victim's sex sometimes influenced these assessments, they often seemed to be based on little more than instinct.

Different occasions, you know, [I handle the transfer differently]. Sometimes I go and get [the money] or sometimes I have [the victim] put it in a bag. Depends [on] the person. I look at a person, and with a person that I think might pull something sneaky, I'll go in there [and get the money myself]. But a person, maybe a woman, I let her put it in there. (No. 02)

[Whether or not I permit the victim to participate in the transfer] depends on the person. I can't explain [what I base my assessment on], I don't know. Seriously, I can't explain that. Instinct, I guess. (No. 10)

Other offenders reported that their decisions about how best to manage the transfer of goods were based on situational contingencies. The most important situational contingency was the presence or absence of an accomplice.

[I tell the victim,] "Put the money in the bag." Or if it's two of us, one person watch the people and the other person put the money in the bag. But if it's just me, I make [the victim] put the money in the bag. (No. 79)

Yet other offenders claimed that victims often were in no state to hand over their valuables. Inevitably, some of them became paralyzed with fear during stickups. When that happened, the offenders had no choice but to effect the transfer on their own.

Sometimes [the victims] be so scared that they be shaking so much that I just got to go and get [the money] out of there. (No. 75)

In a robbery, some of [the victims] be so scared that they just don't move. You just got to dig in they pockets [to get the cash]. (No. 27)

As noted above, all of the crime commission strategies adopted by the offenders are intended, at least in part, to minimize the possibility of victim resistance. Generally speaking, these strategies work very well. Nevertheless, almost all of the armed robbers we talked to said that they occasionally encountered victims who steadfastly refused to comply with their demands.

[I attempted to rob one man who just] said, "Whatever you gonna do, do it." Like I said, you already be so scared, so he said, "I ain't gonna lay down, man. If you gonna kill me, then kill me." (No. 09)

On the parking lot, if you grab somebody and say, "This is a robbery, don't make it a murder," I've had it happen that [the victim just says], "Well, you got to kill me then." (No. 82)

Faced with a recalcitrant victim, most of the offenders responded with severe but nonlethal violence in the hope of convincing the person to cooperate. Often this violence involved smacking or beating the victim about the head with a pistol.

I might smack [victims who refuse to cooperate] with the pistol. . . . I had one person that was just refusing to give me her money. I throwed her down on the ground, no, I made her lay down on the ground, and she refused to lay down. I hit her in the head with the pistol a couple of times and she still refused to give me the money. I took her and beat her again with the pistol and I had her lay down on the floor and stuck the pistol up in her mouth and cocked the trigger, and she still refused to give it to me. I continued to beat her until I beat her unconscious and I got the money myself and left her. (No. 01)

Sometimes I might strike [resistant victims] with that pistol. They usually jump in line because you hit them with that pistol and that blood starts shooting out, they usually get it on [and start cooperating]. (No. 02)

It's happened [that some of my victims initially refuse to hand over their money, but] you would be surprised how cooperative a person will be once he been smashed across the face with a .357 Magnum. (No. 08)

Occasionally, however, it involved shooting the victim in the leg or some other spot unlikely to prove fatal.

[If the person refuses to do what I say] most of the time I just grab my pistol, take the clip out and just slap them. If I see [the victim] trying to get tough, then sometimes I just straight out have to shoot somebody, just shoot them. I ain't never shot nobody in the head or nothing, nowhere that I know would kill them, just shoot them in they leg. Just to let them know that I'm for real [and that they should] just come up off the stuff. (No. 24)

There was one guy, he told me he wasn't coming off with nothing, I'm gonna have to shoot him and all that. So I told him, "You don't think I'll shoot you?" He wanted to play tough . . . so I shot him in the kneecap. I told him to come up off it. He on the ground, he hollering, making all kinds of noise. Now he really have to come up off it. . . . Come to find out, I got gloves on, I go check and there ain't nothing in his pockets or nothing. Nothing in his pockets, all that for nothing! So he played tough and got shot and he didn't have nothing. (C-Loco—No. 26)

While a majority of the armed robbers preferred to use nonlethal violence to subdue resistant victims—presumably because they had moral or legal qualms about killing—several of them admitted to having been involved, at least tangentially, in fatal encounters in the past. One of the female offenders, for instance, described in graphic detail how she had watched from the car while one of her male companions shot and killed an uncooperative robbery victim.

We was in the car and, I didn't get out this time, one of the dudes got out. The [victim], he wasn't gonna let nobody rob him: "Nigger, you got to kill me! You got to kill me!" And that's what happened to him. Just shot him in the head. It was like, "God!" I had never seen that. When [my accomplice] shot him, it wasn't like he was rushing to get away. He shot him, walked back to the car, put the gun back up under the seat and just, you know, we watched [the victim] when he fell, blood was coming out of his mouth, he was shaking or something. (No. 31)

It is important to keep in mind that such incidents are rare and that few of the offenders entered into armed robberies intending to kill or seriously injure their prey. Some of the armed robbers admitted that they probably would abandon an intended offense rather than use deadly force to subdue an uncooperative victim.

> I really ain't gonna shoot nobody. I think a lot of people are like that. I wouldn't shoot nobody myself; if they gave me too much of a problem, I might just take off. (Mike J.—No. 33)

That said, it also must be remembered that the ranks of armed robbers are filled with angry, hostile individuals, many of whom display a strong penchant for sudden violence. Moreover, these volatile characters typically are acting under intense emotional pressure to generate some fast cash by any means necessary in an interactional environment shot through with uncertainty and danger. Is it any wonder that the slightest hint of victim resistance may provoke some of them to respond with potentially deadly force? As one offender explained, "When you're doing stuff like this, you just real edgy; you'll pull the trigger at anything, at the first thing that go wrong."

Making an Escape

Once offenders have accomplished the transfer of goods, it only remains for them to make their getaway. Doing that, however, is harder than it might appear. Up to this point, the offenders have managed to keep victims in check by creating a convincing illusion of impending death. But the successful maintenance of that illusion becomes increasingly more difficult as the time comes for offenders to make good their escape. How can they continue to control victims who are becoming physically more distant from them?

In broad terms, the offenders could effect a getaway in one of two ways; they could leave the scene themselves, or they could stay put and force the victim to flee. Other things being equal, most of them preferred to be the ones to depart. Before doing so, however, they had to make sure that the victim would not attempt to follow them or to raise the alarm. A majority of the offenders responded to this need by deploying verbal threats designed to extend the illusion of impending death just long enough for them to escape unobserved.

I done left people in gangways and alleys and I've told them, "If you come out of this alley, I'm gonna hurt you. Just give me five or ten minutes to get away. If you come out of this alley in three or four minutes, I'm gonna shoot the shit out of you!" (No. 07)

[Before you leave a convenience store robbery], you try to plant enough fear and control [in the victims] that hopefully, instincts again, that they will stay there for a few minutes and take that few minutes to not peek around them corners and not open doors so you can get to the car. (No. 11)

I tell [my victims], "Give me two minutes, if you want nobody to get hurt! My friend is outside in a different car. If anybody comes out, he's got instructions to shoot you." So they stay down, and I walk right out the door [of the shop]. (No. 20)

A few offenders, however, attempted to prolong this illusion indefinitely by threatening to kill their victims if they *ever* mentioned the stickup to anyone.

I done actually took [the victim's] I.D. and told them, "If you call the police, I got your address and everything. I know where you stay at, and if you call the police, I'm gonna come back and kill you!" (No. 01)

[Before I make my getaway, I tell the victim,] "If you say something to the police, if you say anything to anybody, I'm gonna kill you! I be looking for you!" (Yolanda Smith—No. 15)

Some of the armed robbers were uncomfortable relying on verbal threats to dissuade their prey from pursuing them. Instead, they took steps to make it difficult or impossible for victims to leave the crime scene by tying them up or incapacitating them through injury.

[I have tied up my victims] many of times [because] that gives me a chance to get out of the hotel and get in my car, because I always drive, and just go about my business. Cause [the victim] don't think I'm in no car. I change my jeans in the car, take my other stuff off that I work in. (No. 22)

[I hit my victim before I escape so as to] give him less time to call for the police. Especially if it's somebody else's neighborhood [and] we don't know how to get out. You hit him with a bat just to slow his pace. If you hit him in the leg with a bat, he can't walk for a minute; he gonna be limping, gonna try to limp to a pay phone. By then it be fifteen or twenty minutes, we be hitting the highway and on our way back to the southside, where our neighborhood is. (No. 56)

Offenders who targeted men engaged in sexual liaisons often used a less physical but equally effective tactic to incapacitate them—they took their clothes and left them standing naked, too vulnerable and embarrassed to offer chase. This tactic worked so well that it sometimes was employed in other sorts of stickups as well; several armed robbers reported that, before departing, they occasionally forced their drug dealer or gambling victims to strip because doing so substantially reduced the chances of being followed.

While a majority of the offenders wanted to be the first to leave the crime scene, a number of them preferred to order the victim to flee instead. Doing so allowed the offenders to depart in a calm, leisurely manner, thereby minimizing the risk of drawing attention to themselves.

I try not to have to run away. A very important thing that I have learned is that when you run away, too many things can happen running away. Police could just be cruising by and see you running down the street. I just prefer to be able to walk away, which is one of the reasons why I tend, rather than to make an exit, I tell the victim to walk and don't look back: "Walk away, and walk fast!" When they walk, I can make my exit walking. (No. 04)

What is more, forcing the victim to leave first permitted the offenders to escape without worrying about being attacked from behind—a crucial consideration for those unwilling or unable to incapacitate their prey prior to departure.

[Afterward,] I will tell [the victim] to run. You wouldn't just get the stuff and run because he may have a gun and shoot you while you are turning around running or something like that. (No. 34)

Like I said, [before leaving] you just tell [the victims] what direction you want them to go and start walking. You want them to be with their back to you. You don't want to just spin around and turn your back on them. You make sure you put they back to you. Say, "Start walking that way, right now!" They start walking. You stand there five or ten seconds and *then* you go where you are going. (No. 14)

Beyond such instrumental concerns, several of the armed robbers indicated that they forced the victim to flee for expressive reasons as well; it demonstrated their continuing ability to dominate and control the situation. The clearest example of this involved an offender who routinely taunted his victims by ordering them to leave the scene in humiliating circumstances: "I like laughing at what I do, like, I told . . . one dude to take off his clothes. I just do a whole bunch of stuff. Sometimes I'll make a dude crawl away. I'll tell him to crawl all the way up the street. And I'll sit there in the alley watching him crawl and crack up laughing."

HANDLING THE THREAT
OF LEGAL CONSEQUENCES

The actions described above form part of a serious criminal undertaking, and this means that offenders must carry them out under the threat of being caught and punished. Those in our sample were not unmindful of this threat. Almost without exception, they acknowledged that all criminals, no matter how skillful, run some risk of arrest and prosecution. As one noted, "You never know [when you might get caught], freak accident things just happen." While actually engaged in an armed robbery, the offenders employed various methods to handle this prospect mentally so it would not inhibit their ability to offend. They consciously used cognitive techniques that allowed them to "neutralize" the capacity of threatened sanctions to deter an intended offense (Bennett and Wright 1984). This most commonly involved a steadfast refusal to dwell on the chance of being apprehended, which, of course, precluded consideration of the contingent risks of prosecution and punishment (see, e.g., Shover 1996). Nearly two-thirds of the armed robbers we questioned about this matter—forty-nine of seventy-eight—said that during offenses they typically tried to avoid thinking about the possibility of getting caught.

If I think about [the chance of getting caught], I'm not gonna do [the stickup]. So I try not to think about it. (No. 52)

[The risk of getting caught is] just a reality. I know it's a possibility. But I try not to think about that because if I dwell on it too much I may talk myself or scare myself out of doing [the robbery]. (No. 73)

Some of the offenders seemed to find it easy to keep such thoughts out of their minds. In fact, a number of them denied considering the risk of apprehension altogether.

I never think about no chances [of being apprehended]. I just do [the stickup] and get it over with. No hesitation. (No. 25)

I never even think about [getting caught], I just do [the robbery]. I don't think about nothing, I just do it. (No. 38)

This was especially true for those who specialized in robbing drug dealers. After all, one of them reminded us, "Dope dealers can't even call the police."

Other offenders, however, had to work to stop themselves from contemplating the possibility of getting caught. In effect, they had to push any awareness of that risk out of their minds.

I try to keep [thoughts about getting caught] out of my mind. I look at it more on a positive side: getting away. A lot of times it enters my head about getting caught, but I try to kill that thought by saying I can do it; have confidence in pulling the job off. (No. 01)

[The possibility of apprehension] might run through my mind, but I don't retain it. . . . it's like the thought occurs, but I try to block it out. I don't dwell on it. (No. 09)

Several of the armed robbers drank alcohol or took drugs prior to offending in a deliberate attempt to thwart the deterrence potential of official penalties and thereby to facilitate their ability to commit the stickup.

When you get it in your head to do [a stickup] and you get high, you ain't gonna care no more [about the risk of getting caught]. . . . You go under the influence and you don't really trip off of it. (No. 26)

That's why [my partners and I] get high so much. [We] get high and get stupid, then we don't trip off of [the threat of apprehension]. Whatever happens, happens. . . . You just don't care at the time. (No. 81)

Beyond a desire to weaken the deterrent effect of threatened sanctions, quite a few of the offenders had other reasons to avoid thinking about the chance of getting caught. Some felt that dwelling on this matter only served to create anxiety, which impaired concentration and increased the probability of making a mistake. From their perspective, thinking about getting caught could actually be counterproductive.

I do [think about the possibility of apprehension], but I try not to. I put forth an effort to try not to think about that. When I was younger, I would tend to think about the consequences. [But] as you get older, anything that you continue to do, [thinking about the risk is] too much of a distraction. You can't concentrate on doing anything if you are thinking, "What's gonna happen if it doesn't go right?" As time went on, if I had made up my mind to do a robbery, [I decided] to be totally focused on that and nothing else. (No. 04)

You can get caught [on a robbery] easier than a motherfucker, but you can't think about that when you doing it. You think about that, then you be scared and shit, then you be like, "No, let me leave this thing alone before I get caught." By the time you say, "leave him alone," you been shot at by then. . . . You been shot and in jail. (Killer Slob—No. 37)

Other offenders were superstitious and believed that thinking about getting caught, in and of itself, could conjure up the presence of law enforcement.

Everytime you think about [getting caught], the police just come up. . . . Like you just bring it on yourself; if you want to get caught, you think about the police. (No. 42)

I believe that when you think about [the chance of being apprehended], it will happen. I don't think about it. (No. 59)

Some of the armed robbers also tried not to think about getting caught because such thoughts generated an uncomfortably high level of mental anguish. They believed that the best way to prevent this from happening was to forget about the risk and leave matters to fate. One of them put it this way: "I don't really trip off getting caught, man, cause you'll just worry yourself like that." Given that almost all of these offenders perceived themselves not only as being under pressure to obtain money quickly but also as having no lawful means of doing so, this makes sense. Where no viable alternative to crime exists, there clearly is little point in dwelling on the potentially negative consequences of offending. It should come as no surprise, then, to learn that the offenders usually preferred to ignore the possible risk and concentrate instead on the anticipated reward.

The way I think about [the threat of being apprehended] is this: I would rather take a chance on getting caught and getting locked up than running around out here broke and not taking a chance on even trying to get no money. (No. 71)

The fact is that in many cases the offenders effectively had no choice (Shover and Honaker 1992); committing a robbery appeared to be their only realistic option. In consequence, they elected to adopt an optimistic rather than a pessimistic stance toward the outcome of their actions.

Just over one-third of the offenders we interviewed reported that, during their stickups, they typically did think about the possibility of being apprehended. Why did an awareness of this risk not deter them from offending? Perhaps the primary reason can be found in their financial distress, which, in practice, tended to overwhelm their concern about the potential risk (see, e.g., Shover 1996).

Like I said, if I'm broke, I need some money in my pocket. I think about [getting caught], but it go through one ear and go out the other. Walking around broke, man, it's not a good feeling. (No. 78)

[I always think about the possibility of apprehension, but] I guess the need is greater than the fear of getting caught. (No. o8)

Generally speaking, these offenders believed that the chance of getting caught for any given robbery was small and, in the face of the anticipated reward, found it easy to discount this threat. For many of them, this process was facilitated by an inflated opinion of their skill at avoiding detection (see also Walters 1990). The offender quoted below, for example, possessed a lengthy criminal record and already had served a long prison sentence for armed robbery. Nevertheless, he claimed that his criminal expertise likely would keep him safe from arrest. Asked if he considered the possibility of being apprehended, he responded:

Definitely! It depends. I don't know. What I'm really trying to say [is that] if you good at what you doing, you don't care too much cause you figure nine times out of ten you not gonna get caught. (No. 62)

Other offenders who, while committing their stickups, typically thought about getting caught felt that this awareness was beneficial; it helped to concentrate their minds on the need for vigilance and caution.

Yeah, [I think about the risk of apprehension], that's why [I take steps] to make it as limited [a threat] as possible. That's why I [do] all these things I'm [telling you about now]; so I don't have to worry about getting caught. (No. 74)

Still other offenders simply adopted a fatalistic attitude toward the prospect of arrest and prosecution.

Sometimes I do worry about [getting caught], but you know, my thing is, "Well, if I go to prison, then I just go to prison." (Buby—No. 18)

I just think about when I get caught, I just get caught. (George—No. 65)

These individuals clearly were aware that they might be caught, but believed that whether this happened was a matter of luck and largely out of their hands. As they saw it, all one could do was to hope for the best.

Lastly, a number of armed robbers thought about the possibility of apprehension during their stickups but carried on nonetheless because they were not overly concerned. A couple of these offenders believed that they were risking prison or jail sentences so short as not to be worth worrying about.

[If I get caught, I'll probably be sentenced to] about ten years [probation]. I would probably do about a hundred and eighty days' shock [incarceration], let me out, put me on some papers. When you get caught, it depends on what kind of weapon it is. Since it's my first offense, the first time of going to jail, period, they'd put me on a hundred and eighty days' shock and then put me on papers and let me out. (No. 46)

The majority, however, fully expected to get caught "sooner or later" and to receive a lengthy prison sentence. Yet they remained indifferent to threatened sanctions. In fact, some of them seemed almost to welcome prison as a pleasant break from the emotional turmoil and physical dangers that marked their day-to-day existence on the street (see also Fleisher 1995; Shover 1996).

Basically jail fun for real. Most people look at jail [as a bad place]. I look at jail as another place to lay my head at. I might be safer in jail than on the streets. (No. 44)

In short, the offenders realized that by committing robberies they risked being caught and punished. Most of them were able to push this thought out of their minds while engaged in an offense, thereby demonstrating a noteworthy ability to undermine "the legal bind of the law" (Bennett and Wright 1984:116). Undoubtedly, this ability was facilitated by typically being in a state of emotional desperation at the time. Lofland (1969:50) has speculated that all people in this situation have a tendency toward "psychosocial encapsulation," wherein they enter a "qualitatively different state of mind" in which the potentially negative consequences of their actions become attenuated. Indeed, many of the offenders who, during their stickups, did think about getting caught often were driven by financial distress to discount that risk and to focus instead on the anticipated reward. Previous research on offender decision making has largely neglected the impact of motivation on perceptions of risk. This is a serious omission because, in practice, the reason for contemplating a crime in the first place often serves to diminish the perceived threat of official sanctions (see, e.g., Shover 1996).

HANDLING THE GUILT

The fear of legal consequences is not the only psychological mechanism that could dissuade would-be armed robbers from committing a stickup. After all, moral condemnation of robbery is nearly universal. Hence anticipated feelings of guilt also might constrain the lawbreaking of potential offenders. Without doubt, all of the offenders knew that committing armed robbery was frowned upon by the general public. As one observed: "In some warped sort of way . . . I [do] understand the difference between right and wrong." However, a majority of those who commented on the morality of doing stickups—fifty-seven of seventy-seven—claimed they usually experienced no guilt when actually carrying out an offense.

I have never felt no pain for nobody. . . . That's how I was raised up. . . . My father always told me never to feel no pity for nobody. So I don't feel no pity for nobody. (No. 25)

I just don't [feel any guilt]. Ain't no love on the streets. I don't care about nobody. I don't care about nothing but me and my family. (No. 57)

These offenders offered a variety of explanations for their lack of guilt. Many claimed that they needed the money to survive and could not afford to feel sorry for their victims.

I don't have no remorse. They got money. I got to get mine, so I'll take yours. (No. 36)

I don't feel sorry for [my victims] because I ain't got no money and they do. (ALT—No. 41)

There is a danger in accepting this explanation at face value. Remember that most of the offenders spent the money from their stickups on alcohol, drugs, and gambling, not on everyday necessities. Like many street criminals, however, they seemed unable to distinguish between what they merely wanted and what they truly needed for survival (see Walters 1990). This confusion made it easy for them to justify the pursuit of a self-indulgent lifestyle by any means necessary, including armed robbery.

Perhaps not surprisingly, the offenders who specialized in robbing drug dealers or other sorts of lawbreakers typically argued that their victims deserved no sympathy.

No, I don't [feel sorry for my victims]! They don't feel sorry out there selling they dope to the people they selling it to. It's killing people they selling it to. (No. 63)

I don't even think about [feeling guilty] because, like, I feel like a little old woman, like my grandmother or something, that's something different; they done worked for [their money]. But these dudes [I rob], they ain't worked for it, they selling drugs to get it. An innocent old person or something, I got friends that will do it. [But] I don't want to be involved with that. I'm just about getting

out there and getting [drug dealers], the ones that showboat.
(No. 31)

Some of these offenders went so far as to suggest that their
victims might just as easily have been the ones to rob them.

Why feel sorry? [The victims] might try to do you the same way. I
got to get some money. (No. 43)

It would be difficult to overstate the predatory nature of
the street corner culture from which our sample was recruited. And it would be naive to deny that this has a powerful influence on how many of the offenders interpret the experience of victimization. A number of them maintained that
there was no need to feel sorry for their victims; being robbed
was simply one of life's risks—it could happen to them too—
and in the overall scheme of things, was no big deal.

It's like this, you never know, somebody probably do me like that.
That's why we don't feel guilty. It might happen to us. (No. 16)

You know the chance you taking. You could get robbed just as
quick as anybody else could. . . . So it's an even proposition, I think.
(No. 80)

Several of these offenders had been robbed themselves and
used this to justify their lack of compassion for those they
victimized.

I just don't feel sorry [for my victims]. I been robbed before and I
feel like, if somebody rob me, they ain't gonna feel sorry when they
rob me, so I don't feel sorry for nobody. (No. 48)

No, [I never feel guilty during my stickups] cause when I got
robbed, they didn't feel sorry for me. (No. 64)

Finally, there was one armed robber who said he did not
feel guilty because his victims brought offenses on themselves by ostentatiously displaying their wealth. Such people,

in his mind, were unworthy of sympathy. As he put it, "You shouldn't be flashing. You walking around with big gold chains, rings, and all that, you deserve to get got!"

For our purposes, the important point is that during their robberies a majority of the offenders could not be constrained by a guilty conscience; they simply did not have one. That said, some of them reported feelings of guilt immediately following a stickup, especially if the victim had been hurt.

I've felt guilty because I've had to strike somebody, that's the only time I ever feel guilty. I don't feel guilty about taking the money. Having to strike someone really makes me feel guilty. (No. 06)

I'm doing something I have to do, [but] I think about it after the fact. I feel sorry if [the victim] got fucked up pretty bad. (No. 47)

Such feelings, however, had a tendency to dissipate quickly so that, when the need to commit another stickup arose, they no longer carried much emotional force for the offenders.

[After my brother shot one of our victims] I was like, he didn't really have to shoot him. But then it was like, "Well, you shot him. What can you do about it [now]?" (No. 18)

When we have to hurt people, then we really be feeling, "Why did we shoot that dude?" [But then] one of [us] will say, "Man, that's on them, he should have followed our instructions." (No. 67)

Twenty of the seventy-seven offenders who addressed the issue of guilt reported that they usually did have pangs of conscience during their robberies. Given the financial pressure they were under, however, the guilt experienced was not powerful enough to prevent them from offending.

Yeah, [I feel guilty]. . . . I just wish that I had a job that I can go to so I wouldn't have to do stupid shit like this; people work too hard for their money. But I got to have some too. I can't survive without no money. I wish I could apologize, but realistically that's not gonna happen. (No. 76)

In general, then, feelings of guilt were in short supply among the armed robbers we interviewed; almost three-quarters of them claimed that their consciences did not bother them at all during offenses. These offenders knew full well that robbery was wrong. Nevertheless, they typically did not pause to consider the moral implications of their actions while actually contemplating an offense. This, in turn, facilitated the initial decision to commit a stickup by enhancing its "subjective availability" (Lofland 1969:84). After all, other things being equal, most people are reluctant to engage in activities that they consciously consider to be morally repugnant. But in the real world things are not always equal. This explains how those offenders who usually did feel guilty came to commit their crimes; their moral qualms were overridden by situational pressures, most notably the need to get money quickly so that they could continue partying.

SUMMARY

The offenders in our study typically compel the cooperation of intended victims through the creation of a convincing illusion of impending death. They create this illusion by catching would-be victims off guard and then using tough talk, a fierce demeanor, and the display of a deadly weapon to scare them into unquestioning compliance. The goal is to maintain the illusion for as long as possible—ideally beyond the offense itself—without having to make good on the threat. This is easier said than done. Armed robbery, after all, is an interactive event, and victims may fail to behave in the expected fashion. When this happens the offenders usually respond with severe but nonlethal violence, relying on brute force to bring the victims' behavior back into line with their expectations. Few of them enter offenses wanting to kill their victims, but some clearly are prepared to resort to deadly force if need be.

The armed robbers have to commit their stickups under the threat of getting caught and punished. During their crimes most of them consciously avoid dwelling on the risk of apprehension. In doing so, they undercut the deterrence value of threatened sanctions and thus can offend unimpeded by concerns about the potentially negative consequences. Some of the offenders typically do think about the possibility of getting caught but proceed anyway because the anticipated reward overwhelms the perceived risk. It bears reiterating that they almost invariably are contemplating their offenses in response to financial pressure. The attractiveness of the expected payoff is bound to be enhanced in such circumstances. Add to this the offenders' knowledge that the chance of being arrested for any given stickup is low, and it is easy to appreciate how the weighing of risks and rewards results in a decision to offend.

The offenders clearly understand that armed robbery is morally wrong. Nevertheless, most of them experience no guilt whatsoever during their stickups. Those who do have moral qualms typically perceive themselves as having little choice but to offend, guilty conscience notwithstanding. In either case, the end result is the same: at the time of actually contemplating their crimes the armed robbers cannot realistically be dissuaded from offending by internalized moral beliefs.

By and large, the offenders do not view themselves as having the luxury of freedom of choice in committing their stickups. Rather, they typically see their decisions to offend as emanating from a desperate financial need that cannot easily be met through more conventional means. In a sense, the pressure of their immediate situation attenuates the perceptual link between offending and the risk of incurring sanctions; they enter a state of "encapsulation" (Lofland 1969: 50–54) in which all that matters is dealing with the present crisis. This will come as bad news to policymakers because high offender motivation further complicates the already difficult task of crime prevention.

5 Preventing Armed Robbery

The physical dangers that we confronted in doing the research for this book were nothing compared to the emotional toll exacted on us by the nature of our work. Even now, nearly two years after leaving the field, we continue to ask ourselves whether it was ethical to study active armed robbers in a real-world setting. There is no easy answer to that question, though we would think twice before undertaking a similar project in the future. By studying armed robbers in their "natural habitat," we clearly learned some things about their decision making that could not be discovered by interviewing prisoners. But almost everyone, conservatives and liberals alike, would agree that such offenders represent a serious social menace and belong behind bars. No matter how laudable the research goal, one quickly grows weary of paying armed robbers to provide information about their stickups and then watching them walk away to rob again. All of this, however, is academic; for better or worse, our study is long since completed. The challenge now is to put that study to good use by mining it for insights that ultimately might contribute to the prevention and control of armed robbery.

JOB CREATION

Our research paints a portrait of armed robbers who, in the immediate situation of their crimes, perceive themselves as having little choice but to commit a stickup. This suggests that one possible strategy for preventing their offenses might be to keep them from getting into the criminogenic situation in the first place. Such a strategy will be effective only to the extent that it undermines the strong emotional attachment of the offenders to street culture (see also Moran 1996). Most of their lawbreaking, after all, is motivated directly by a desperate desire to participate in and sustain various illicit activities promoted by that culture. Weakening the commitment of the offenders to street life, however, is a tall order, with formidable obstacles to success. If we take as a starting point what the offenders told us, job creation would seem to be the most promising method of tempting them away from the street corner.

Quite a few said that they wanted to work and would slow down or stop offending altogether if someone gave them a good-paying job. Creating such jobs in the face of a declining manufacturing base and fierce competition from cheaper domestic and foreign labor markets is a daunting, long-term task (Wilson 1996). But even if this were accomplished, it is not clear that the offenders would be able to take advantage of the new employment opportunities. Not only are the majority of them poorly educated and unskilled, but many are also unreliable, suffering from drug or alcohol problems, and resistant to following instructions or taking orders. Moreover, by definition, all of the offenders are of questionable trustworthiness. These are not personal attributes highly sought after in a prospective employee. Nor is it clear that, when push comes to shove, the offenders actually would be willing to work for a living; after a lifetime of hustling, any legitimate job realistically available to them almost certainly would be perceived by many as an unacceptably slow and tedious way to generate cash.

None of this should be taken to suggest that expanded employment opportunities will necessarily be ineffective in reducing robbery rates in general, only that we are dubious about the impact of a job creation program on the offending of those already committed to the criminogenic norms and values of street culture. High concentrations of chronically jobless people undoubtedly help to create the anomic conditions under which street culture thrives by disrupting the ordered existence imposed on individuals by the world of work. As Wilson (1996:73) has observed:

Work is not simply a way to make a living and support one's family. It also constitutes a framework for daily behavior and patterns of interaction because it imposes disciplines and regularities. Thus, in the absence of regular employment, a person lacks not only a place in which to work and the receipt of regular income but also a coherent organization of the present—that is, a system of concrete expectations and goals. Regular employment provides the anchor for the spatial and temporal aspects of daily life. It determines where you are going to be and when you are going to be there. In the absence of regular employment, life, including family life, becomes less coherent.

It follows that successfully breaking the cycle of persistent joblessness that characterizes most high-crime inner-city neighborhoods might eventually lead to a reduction in robbery by starving the local street culture of new recruits. Wilson (1996:228) speculates that one way to accomplish this would be to create public-sector jobs that pay poor, low-skilled workers subminimum wages to "produce goods and provide services that are not available in the private sector." Whatever the potential long-term benefits for crime reduction of such a scheme might be, it remains doubtful that many of the current armed robbers in our sample would be prepared to subordinate their immediate desires to the demands of any job, let alone one that paid less than the minimum wage.

DETERRENCE AND INCAPACITATION

Threatened criminal penalties for armed robbery already are severe; there is little reason to believe that increasing them will deter the offenders from committing further stickups. Recall that their decisions to offend typically are made in circumstances where they perceive themselves both as under pressure to act quickly and as having no realistic alternative to robbery. Combine this with the fact that the armed robbers know from experience that the chance of getting caught for any given offense is extremely small, and it becomes clear why the threat of sanctions, no matter how harsh, is unlikely to dissuade them from doing more stickups in the future. Increased penalties for armed robbery might serve as successful deterrents only if accompanied by detection rates so dramatically improved as to extinguish offenders' perception of the offense as a realistically available option. It is hard to imagine that an improvement in robbery clearance rates of that magnitude can be achieved within the foreseeable future.

If the offenders cannot easily be deterred, those who are caught still can be incapacitated, that is, imprisoned for a long period of time to prevent them from preying on law-abiding citizens (see, e.g., Fleisher 1995). This has been the nation's central crime control strategy for more than a decade, and it may in part be responsible for recent reductions in violent and property offense rates across the country (Federal Bureau of Investigation 1995). But there is at least one serious drawback to relying exclusively on a strategy of incapacitation to control armed robbery; it leaves intact the offenders' commitment to the criminogenic norms and values of street culture. Thus many offenders continue to commit robberies while in prison, often in pursuit of illicit forms of action similar to those that drove them toward crime on the outside (e.g., drug taking). While proponents of harsh punishment might be untroubled by this, Shover (1996:181) has warned that our heavy reliance on lengthy prison sentences to the neglect of long-term strategies designed to undermine the sociocultural conditions that breed criminal motivation could well backfire:

When persistent [offenders] are incarcerated, the results sometimes are different from those intended by advocates of punishment. Perceptions of its harshness are undermined by experience with imprisonment, particularly reassurance that it can be endured. Persistent [lawbreakers] rationalize crime and believe they can perfect criminal techniques and become successful. It can be argued, of course, that if prison conditions generally were more austere and regimented, surely fewer [offenders] would react to the experience in this way. If confinement does not put sufficient fear into inmates, perhaps it is because the regimen is too easy and an increase in unpleasantness is needed. . . . No one can say confidently what the net result of such a development would be, but it is useful to note that enduring extremely harsh or brutal treatment can reassure some prisoners even as it kindles dangerous emotions. I refer specifically to embitterment, anger, and the desire to wreak revenge. This reaction can crystallize and strengthen a conception of oneself as a person who has been treated unfairly by authorities. Advocates and supporters of America's return to harsh crime-control policies have paid scant attention to the emotional consequences of the programs spun off of them.

Before rushing headlong to embrace the continued or increased use of incapacitation to control armed robbery, we should pause to consider the future: What will happen when, possessing little more than a prison record and the clothes on their back, today's convicted armed robbers return in droves to the mean streets whence they came?

REDUCING VICTIM VULNERABILITY

Given that undermining the motivational wellsprings of offender behavior is extremely difficult, it may be more practical, at least in the short term, to concentrate our efforts on reducing the vulnerability of potential victims. Although some people undoubtedly will dismiss such a suggestion as tantamount to victim blaming, it is worth noting that efforts to change victim behavior are not fundamentally different from widely accepted strategies designed to make inanimate targets (e.g., houses) less attractive to would-be offenders. Besides, robbery victims often are not blameless; more than half of the offenders in our sample typically targeted people who themselves were involved in various sorts of lawbreaking. And while seasoned drug sellers clearly understand that their activities put them at increased risk for being robbed, the same cannot confidently be said about some of their less streetwise middle-class customers. Nor do men seeking the services of a prostitute universally appreciate that this pursuit entails a substantial chance of robbery. It is ironic that the need to educate these men about the importance of condom use to avoid AIDS and other sexually transmitted diseases is widely acknowledged, but virtually no thought is given to informing them about the risk of becoming a crime victim. There is an obvious need for an anticrime information campaign targeted explicitly on novice and occasional petty lawbreakers, who are not sufficiently familiar with the ways of the street to comprehend fully the considerable risk of criminal victimization. Such lawbreakers might well decide to behave differently if they were made more aware of this risk.

Admittedly, a substantial percentage of the offenders we interviewed usually robbed people who were engaged in perfectly legitimate activities (e.g., shopping, cashing a check, or bar hopping). But even here there may be scope to reduce the vulnerability of such people by providing them with information about what armed robbers look for when choosing their victims. As noted in chapter 3, most would-be robbers are attracted to victims by outward signs of wealth. Thus people should be reminded not to wear expensive jewelry or display large amounts of cash in public. This advice is especially applicable to individuals who frequent places in and around socially disorganized areas already characterized by high rates of robbery, where there is likely to be a concentration of offenders on the lookout for potentially lucrative targets. It also seems sensible to warn people against the use of automatic teller machines late at night. Remember the words of one of our subjects: "Them instant tellers, I love that!" This respondent no doubt was expressing a view held by many other armed robbers as well.

What should individuals do if they are confronted by an armed robber? The results of our study suggest that immediate cooperation represents their best chance of avoiding serious injury or death. Most of the offenders we spoke to said that they typically responded to any indication of victim resistance with severe violence; a few even admitted to involvement in the killing of one or more recalcitrant victims. The problem, from the victims' perspective, is that offenders tend to define cooperation quite narrowly and, given the interactional character of the robbery event, that definition is likely to shift numerous times as the offense unfolds. As a result, it often is difficult for victims to discern precisely how an assailant expects them to behave at any particular point in time. Obviously, we cannot offer a fail-safe strategy for overcoming this difficulty. One thing, however, is clear: the vast majority of armed robbers do not want victims to look directly at them for fear of being identified. Unless the attacker demands otherwise, we would strongly advise robbery victims to avert their eyes during offenses.

SITUATIONAL CHANGE

It would be a mistake to expect dramatic results from a robbery prevention publicity campaign seeking to persuade potential victims to change their behavior. Campaigns advising people to take security precautions have proven to be largely ineffective (for a review, see Riley and Mayhew 1980). This leads us to consider one last strategy for preventing armed robbery: altering the situational characteristics that make stickups possible. The offenders we interviewed had clear

ideas about what sorts of physical settings were most conducive to robbery, namely, places shielded from public view
with good escape routes. Thus, other things being equal, any
situational change that serves to increase surveillability (e.g.,
improved lighting) or to decrease access (e.g., entrance and
exit restrictions) should make an area less attractive to armed
robbers. Locations in and around commercial establishments
devoted to cash-intensive activities—areas high on offenders' lists of likely hunting grounds—are perhaps the most
obvious candidates for such changes.

Many cash-intensive businesses, both public and private,
already have made costly physical design changes in an attempt to prevent their employees and customers from being
robbed. While this may or may not be effective in reducing
the likelihood of crime in a specific location, as a general robbery prevention strategy it is woefully inadequate. Physical
design changes have little or no effect on offender motivation; the pool of would-be armed robbers remains as large as
ever. This opens up the strong possibility that stickups pre-
vented in one spot will merely be committed elsewhere, perhaps on the periphery of the protected site. Potential victims,
after all, still must enter and exit that site to conduct their
business.

There is one situational change with the potential to strike
at the heart of offender motivation: the complete elimination
of cash from the economy in favor of a debit and credit
card–based system of electronic monetary transfers. In conducting our research, we were struck time and again by the
central role of cash in shaping the armed robbers' decision
making throughout the offense. Obtaining cash is critically
important to most of these offenders because, without it, the
pursuit of street action is all but impossible. For obvious reasons, purveyors of illicit drugs, gambling, and street corner
sex do not accept payment by check or credit card. Thus these
financial instruments currently are valuable to offenders only
to the extent that they can be employed to generate cash by

either selling them to fellow criminals or using them to purchase legitimate goods for resale on the street. This requires offenders to expend additional time and effort and exposes them to increased risk. As a result, many armed robbers already regard the theft of checkbooks and credit cards to be more trouble than it is worth. In a truly cashless society, the vast majority of them almost surely would come to view these instruments as having no practical value whatsoever.

It is unlikely that the criminogenic activities that underpin and promote street culture could continue to flourish in a cashless society. How, for example, would street-level dope dealers make payment for their drug shipments? For that matter, what would their customers use to pay them? Similar questions might be asked about prostitution, illicit gambling, or the illegal sale of firearms, all of which currently depend on a steady infusion of untraceable cash. Undermining such activities by choking off the cash that fuels them should lead to a dramatic reduction in many forms of predatory crime, including armed robbery, and perhaps deal a death blow to street life itself.

Although the idea of a cashless society may seem far-fetched, there are clear signs that we are heading in this direction. In direct response to the threat of armed robbery, for instance, many small retail businesses have restricted the amount of cash accessible to employees and have prohibited customers from using large bills to pay for purchases. Likewise, public transportation systems across the country increasingly have moved to "exact fare" payment systems, thereby making it unnecessary for drivers and other personnel to carry cash. From measures such as these, it is but a short step to eliminating cash altogether and replacing it with debit or credit cards. Already it is possible to use either one of these cash alternatives to pay for a public telephone call or purchase gasoline.

Many upper- and middle-class people currently operate in an essentially cashless economy, carrying little or no money and relying almost exclusively on checkbooks or credit cards to conduct their day-to-day business. Recall that some of the offenders in our sample were unwilling to rob prosperous-looking individuals for just this reason. But lower-class people often do not have bank accounts or credit cards and continue to pay for goods and services in cash. This makes them attractive robbery targets—a particularly acute problem for the urban poor, who frequently live in close proximity to would-be offenders.

The vulnerability of the urban poor to armed robbery is exemplified best by offenders who hang around local check-cashing establishments and prey on welfare recipients after they have cashed their government assistance checks (see chapter 3). Observing this, it occurred to us that one promising approach to the prevention of armed robbery in the inner city would be to replace welfare checks with debit cards (complete with personal identification numbers) that either do not allow cash withdrawals or else restrict them to a few dollars a day. The use of such cards could be limited to approved purchases and payments (e.g., food, rent, utilities), thereby minimizing the misuse of welfare funds. This, in turn, should help to bleed money out of neighborhood drug markets and may contribute to a reduction in drug-related violence. These would be important secondary benefits of such a scheme given current nationwide concerns with welfare reform, illicit drug use, and violent crime. The primary value of a debit card–based system of welfare payments, however, lies in its potential for reducing robbery victimization among the people who can least afford it, the nation's urban poor.

APPENDIX

Code#	Alias*	Sex	Race	Age	Age at First Robbery	Robberies in Last Month	Previous Robbery Arrests	Previous Robbery Convictions
01	Melvin Walker	M	B	37	17	4	Y	Y
02	Wyman Danger	M	B	46	21	2	Y	N
03	Marko Maze	M	B	41	17	2	Y	Y
04	Slick Going	M	B	47	18	***	Y	Y
05	Cedric Rhone	M	B	37	14	3	Y	Y
06	James Williams	M	B	51	14	***	Y	N
07	Bennie Simmons	M	B	44	20	***	Y	Y
08	Tony Wright	M	B	43	25	***	Y	Y
09	Bob Jones	M	B	39	17	1	Y	Y
10	Rudy	M	B	39	13	1	Y	Y
11	Robert Jones	M	B	46	14	1	Y	Y
12	Robert Lee Davis	M	B	42	19	1	Y	Y
13	John Lee	M	B	32	17	2	Y	Y
14	James Minor	M	B	47	17	***	Y	Y
15	Yolanda Smith	F	B	22	19	4	Y	N
16	Vincent Ray	M	B	25	16	3	Y	N
17	CMW	F	B	16	14	1	N	NA
18	Buby	F	B	17	17	4	N	NA
19	Larry Washington	M	B	35	15	5	Y	Y
20	Larry Brooks	M	B	38	15	1	Y	Y

Code#	Alias*	Sex	Race	Age	Age at First Robbery	Robberies in Last Month	Previous Robbery Arrests	Previous Robbery Convictions
21	Little Bill	M	B	20	18	1	N	NA
22	Jayzo	F	B	43	27	2	Y	Y
23	Jack Alone	M	B	15	14	6	Y	N
24	Cooper	M	B	17	13	4	Y	Y
25	Looney	M	B	18	13	3	Y	Y
26	C-Loco	M	B	20	14	***	N	NA
27	James Love	M	B	18	14	1	N	NA
28	Redwood	M	B	19	14	2	Y	Y
29	Van Pelet	M	W	30	30	***	Y	N
30	T-Bone	M	B	19	16	2	N	NA
31	Ne-Ne	F	B	20	16	1	N	NA
32	Quick	F	B	19	15	***	Y	N
33	Mike J.	M	B	18	17	1	N	NA
34	Damon Jones	M	B	21	19	1	N	NA
35	Bounty Hunter	M	B	18	13	8	Y	Y
36	Menace	M	B	16	14	3	N	NA
37	Killer Slob	M	B	16	13	4	N	NA
38	Loco	M	B	20	17	2	Y	Y
39	Tish	F	W	18	17	3	N	NA
40	Lisa Jones	F	W	18	17	5	N	NA
41	ALT	M	B	15	14	7	Y	N
42	Thugg	M	B	15	12	2	N	NA

43	K-Money #1	M	B	18	14	3	Y	Y
44	Andrew	M	B	19	8	10	Y	N
45	Red Man	M	B	19	16	10	Y	Y
46	Big Prod	M	B	19	18	1	N	NA
47	John Brown	M	B	34	18	15	N	NA
48	Wallie Cleaver	M	B	25	17	2	Y	Y
49	Nicole Simpson	F	B	26	17	2	N	NA
50	Swoop	M	B	17	16	1	N	NA
51	Woods	M	B	18	17	***	N	NA
52	Taz	M	B	17	14	1	N	NA
53	Bigtops	M	B	17	15	2	Y	N
54	Ms. Berry	F	B	19	17	2	Y	N
55	James Scott	M	B	18	13	2	N	NA
56	Antwon Wright	M	B	19	14	1	Y	N
57	Libbie Jones	F	B	18	12	1	Y	N
58	Janet Outlaw	F	B	20	15	5	Y	N
59	Kid Kutt	M	B	24	12	4	Y	N
60	K-Money #2	M	B	17	16	1	Y	N
61	Frank Nitti #1	M	B	16	11	25	Y	Y
62	Joe Thomas	M	B	39	13	2	Y	Y
63	Frank Nitti #2	M	B	22	15	10	N	NA
64	Carlos Reed	M	B	24	15	3	N	NA
65	George	M	B	34	17	1	N	NA
66	Beano	M	B	18	16	1	Y	N

Code#	Alias*	Sex	Race	Age	Age at First Robbery	Robberies in Last Month	Previous Robbery Arrests	Previous Robbery Convictions
67	Syco	M	B	17	12	3	Y	N
68	Lavon Carter	M	B	37	20	2	Y	Y
69	Robert Gibson	M	B	44	20	1	Y	Y
70	W. Joe Murphy	M	B	49	19	1	Y	N
71	Larry Pate	M	B	38	17	1	Y	Y
72	Nick	M	B	28	16	2	Y	Y
73	Red	M	B	44	15	1	N	NA
74	Fred Harris	M	B	32	16	1	Y	Y
75	Vick Smith	M	B	39	14	3	Y	N
76	Ray Holmes	M	B	35	20	1	Y	Y
77	Treason Taylor	M	B	22	18	2	N	NA
78	Bill Williams	M	B	37	18	2	N	NA
79	Black	M	B	21	16	1	N	NA
80	Burle	M	B	49	17	3	Y	Y
81	Tony Brown	M	B	35	20	4	Y	Y
82	Richard L. Brown	M	B	47	14	1	Y	Y
83	Lisa Wood	F	B	37	18	1	Y	Y
84	Prauch	M	B	36	22	1	Y	N
85	Kim Brown	F	B	37	28	***	Y	Y
86	K.C.	M	B	36	28	1	Y	N

* This alias was chosen by the offender. In cases where two offenders chose the same alias, we numbered them chronologically.

*** No robberies committed in the month preceding the interview.

References

Anderson, E. 1994. "The Code of the Streets." *Atlantic Monthly* 273:81–94.

Bennett, J. 1981. *Oral History and Delinquency: The Rhetoric of Criminology*. Chicago: University of Chicago Press.

Bennett, T., and R. Wright. 1984. *Burglars on Burglary: Prevention and the Offender*. Aldershot, England: Gower.

Berreman, G. 1972. "Behind Many Masks: Ethnography and Impression Management." In *Hindus of the Himalayas*, ed. G. Berreman, xvii–lvii. Berkeley and Los Angeles: University of California Press.

Black, D. 1983. "Crime as Social Control." *American Sociological Review* 48:34–45.

Blumstein, A., and J. Cohen. 1979. "Estimation of Individual Crime Rates from Arrest Records." *Journal of Criminal Law and Criminology* 70:561–85.

Bottoms, A., and P. Wiles. 1992. "Explanations of Crime and Place." In *Crime, Policing and Place: Essays in Environmental Criminology*, ed. D. Evans, N. Fyfe, and D. Herbert, 11–35. London: Routledge.

Brantingham, P., and P. Brantingham. 1981. *Environmental Criminology*. Beverly Hills, Calif.: Sage.

Conklin, J. 1972. *Robbery*. Philadelphia: Lippincott.

Cook, P. 1991. "Robbery in the United States: Analysis of Recent Trends and Patterns." In *Violence: Patterns, Causes, Public*

Policy, ed. N. Weiner, M. Zahn, and R. Sagi, 85–98. New York: Harcourt, Brace and Jovanovich.

Cornish, D. 1994. "Crimes as Scripts." In *Environmental Criminology and Crime Analysis*, ed. D. Zahm and P. Cromwell, 30–45. Coral Gables, Fla.: Florida Criminal Justice Executive Institute.

Cromwell, P., J. Olson, and D. Avary. 1991. *Breaking and Entering: An Ethnographic Analysis of Burglary*. Newbury Park, Calif.: Sage.

Davis, P. 1995. "If You Came This Way." Interview. *All Things Considered*, National Public Radio, 12 October.

Decker, S., and B. Van Winkle. 1996. *Life in the Gang: Family, Friends, and Violence*. New York: Cambridge University Press.

Decker, S., R. Wright, A. Redfern, and D. Smith. 1993. "A Woman's Place is in the Home: Females and Residential Burglary." *Justice Quarterly* 10:143–62.

Einstadter, W. 1969. "The Social Organization of Armed Robbery." *Social Problems* 17:64–83.

Ekblom, P. 1987. *Preventing Robberies at Sub-Post Offices: An Evaluation of a Security Initiative*. Crime Prevention Unit Paper no. 9. England and Wales: Home Office.

Farrington, D. 1993. "Motivations for Conduct Disorder and Delinquency." *Development and Psychopathology* 5:225–41.

Federal Bureau of Investigation. 1995. *Crime in the United States 1994*. Washington, D.C.: U.S. Government Printing Office.

Feeney, F. 1986. "Robbers as Decision-Makers." In *The Reasoning Criminal: Rational Choice Perspectives on Offending*, ed. D. Cornish and R. Clarke, 53–71. New York: Springer-Verlag.

Figgie International. 1988. *The Figgie Report, Part VI: The Business of Crime*. Richmond, Va.: Figgie International.

Fleisher, M. 1995. *Beggars and Thieves: Lives of Urban Street Criminals*. Madison: University of Wisconsin Press.

Gabor, T., et al. 1987. *Armed Robber: Cops, Robbers, and Victims*. Springfield, Ill.: Thomas.

Geis, G. 1994. Foreword. In R. Wright and S. Decker, *Burglars on the Job: Streetlife and Residential Break-ins*, ix–xii. Boston: Northeastern University Press.

Glassner, B., and C. Carpenter. 1985. "The Feasibility of an Ethnographic Study of Property Offenders: A Report Prepared for the National Institute of Justice." Mimeograph. Washington, D.C.: National Institute of Justice.

Hacker, A. 1992. *Two Nations: Black and White, Separate, Hostile, Unequal*. New York: Scribners.

Hagedorn, J. 1988. *People and Folks*. Chicago: Lake View Press.

———. 1990. "Back in the Field Again: Gang Research in the Nineties." In *Gangs in America*, ed. R. Huff, 240–59. Newbury Park, Calif.: Sage.

Hobbs, D. 1995. *Bad Business: Professional Crime in Modern Britain*. New York: Oxford University Press.

Irwin, J. 1972. "Participant Observation of Criminals." In *Research on Deviance*, ed. J. Douglas, 117–37. New York: Free Press.

Katz, J. 1988. *Seductions of Crime: Moral and Sensual Attractions in Doing Evil*. New York: Basic Books.

———. 1991. "The Motivation of the Persistent Robber." In *Crime and Justice: A Review of Research*, ed. M. Tonry, 277–305. Chicago: University of Chicago Press.

———. 1995. Review of *Burglars on the Job: Streetlife and Residential Break-ins*, by R. Wright and S. Decker. *Contemporary Sociology* 24:798–99.

Kornhauser, R. 1978. *Social Sources of Delinquency: An Appraisal of Analytic Models*. Chicago: University of Chicago Press.

Lauritsen, J., R. Sampson, and J. Laub. 1991. "The Link between Offending and Victimization among Adolescents." *Criminology* 29:265–92.

Lejeune, R. 1977. "The Management of a Mugging." *Urban Life* 6:123–48.

Lemert, E. 1953. "An Isolation and Closure Theory of Naive Check Forgery." *Journal of Criminal Law, Criminology, and Police Science* 44:296–307.

Lofland, J. 1969. *Deviance and Identity*. Englewood Cliffs, N.J.: Prentice-Hall.

Loftin, C. 1986. "Assaultive Violence as a Contagious Social Process." *Bulletin of the New York Academy of Medicine* 62:550–55.

Luckenbill, D. 1981. "Generating Compliance: The Case of Robbery." *Urban Life* 10:25–46.

McCall, G. 1978. *Observing the Law*. New York: Free Press.

Merry, S. 1981. *Urban Danger: Life in a Neighborhood of Strangers*. Philadelphia: Temple University Press.

Moore, J. 1991. *Going Down to the Barrio: Homeboys and Homegirls in Change*. Philadelphia: Temple University Press.

Moran, R. 1996. "Bringing Rational Choice Theory Back to Reality." *Journal of Criminal Law and Criminology* 86:1147–60.

Murray, C. 1983. "The Physical Environment and Community Control of Crime." In *Crime and Public Policy*, ed. J. Q. Wilson, 107–22. San Francisco: ICS Press.

National Research Council. 1993. *Understanding and Preventing Violence*. Washington, D.C.: National Academy Press.

Oliver, W. 1994. *The Violent Social World of Black Men*. New York: Lexington Books.

Padilla, F. 1992. *The Gang as an American Enterprise*. New Brunswick, N.J.: Rutgers University Press.

Polsky, N. 1969. *Hustlers, Beats, and Others*. Garden City, N.J.: Anchor Books.

Reaves, B. 1993. *Using NIBRS Data to Analyze Violent Crime*. Bureau of Justice Statistics Technical Report. Washington, D.C.: U.S. Department of Justice.

Reiss, A., Jr. 1986. "Why Are Communities Important in Understanding Crime?" In *Communities and Crime*, ed. A. Reiss Jr. and M. Tonry, 1–33. Chicago: University of Chicago Press.

Rengert, G., and J. Wasilchick. 1989. *Space, Time and Crime: Ethnographic Insights into Residential Burglary*. Final Report Submitted to the National Institute of Justice, Office of Justice Programs. Washington, D.C.: U.S. Department of Justice.

Riley, D., and P. Mayhew. 1980. *Crime Prevention Publicity: An Assessment*. London: Her Majesty's Stationery Office.

Saint Louis Metropolitan Police Department. 1994. *Annual Report, 1993/1994*.

Sanders, W. 1994. *Gangbangs and Drive-bys: Grounded Culture and Juvenile Gang Violence*. New York: Aldine.

Scheff, T. 1990. *Microsociology: Discourse, Emotion, and Social Structure.* Chicago: University of Chicago Press.

Shover, N. 1991. "Burglary." In *Crime and Justice: An Annual Review of Research,* ed. M. Tonry, 14:73–113. Chicago: University of Chicago Press.

———. 1996. *Great Pretenders: Pursuits and Careers of Persistent Thieves.* Boulder, Colo.: Westview.

Shover, N., and D. Honaker. 1992. "The Socially-Bounded Decision Making of Persistent Property Offenders." *Howard Journal of Criminal Justice* 31:276–93.

Skogan, W. 1986. "Fear of Crime and Neighborhood Change." In *Communities and Crime,* ed. A. Reiss Jr. and M. Tonry, 203–30. Chicago: University of Chicago Press.

Sluka, J. 1990. "Participant Observation in Violent Social Contexts." *Human Organization* 49:114–26.

Sommers, I., and D. Baskin. 1993. "The Situational Context of Violent Female Offending." *Journal of Research in Crime and Delinquency* 30:136–62.

Stein, M., and G. McCall. 1994. "Home Ranges and Daily Rounds: Uncovering Community among Urban Nomads." *Research in Community Sociology* 1:77–94.

Sudman, S. 1976. *Applied Sampling.* New York: Academic Press.

Tunnell, K. 1992. *Choosing Crime: The Criminal Calculus of Property Offenders.* Chicago: Nelson/Hall.

Van Maanen, J. 1988. *Tales of the Field: On Writing Ethnography.* Chicago: University of Chicago Press.

Walters, G. 1990. *The Criminal Lifestyle: Patterns of Serious Criminal Conduct.* Newbury Park, Calif.: Sage.

Watters, J., and P. Biernacki. 1989. "Targeted Sampling: Options for the Study of Hidden Populations." *Social Problems* 36:416–30.

West, W. 1980. "Access to Adolescent Deviants and Deviance." In *Fieldwork Experience: Qualitative Approaches to Social Research,* ed. W. Shaffir, R. Stebbins, and A. Turowitz, 31–44. New York: St. Martin's Press.

Wilson, J. Q., and B. Boland. 1976. "Crime." In *The Urban Predicament*, ed. W. Gorham and N. Glazer, 179–230. Washington, D.C.: Urban Institute.

Wilson, W. J. 1996. *When Work Disappears: The World of the New Urban Poor*. New York: Knopf.

Wright, R., and S. Decker. 1994. *Burglars on the Job: Streetlife and Residential Break-ins*. Boston: Northeastern University Press.

Index

Small business: robbery and, 90
"Snowball" sampling technique,
17–24
Spontaneity: in street culture, 44
Status, 16; in criminal motivation,
40–42
"Stick candy men," 16
Stickups (*see also* Armed robbery):
accomplices in, 99, 101, 102, 111,
112; approach to victim in, 97–
103; character of, 95–96; communication with victim in, 103–5,
136; firearms in, 105–7; get-
aways, 115–18; lethal violence in,
7, 114, 128, 136; nonlethal violence in, 7, 9–10, 87, 113–15,
116–17, 128, 136; threat of death
in, 96, 103, 104, 107, 116, 128;
transfer of goods (property) in,
107–15
Street culture, 59; drug use in, 39,
49; role of cash in, 137–38; unemployment and, 132; values of,
37–40, 41, 42, 44, 47
Street justice: in criminal motivation, 58
Street robbery, 15–16, 61–62; risk
assessment, 78–81; targeting
criminal victims, 62–71, 93–94;
targeting location, 73–81, 87;
targeting noncriminal victims,
72–73, 81–88, 94
Supermarkets, 78, 90

Tagging: in data selection and
analysis, 29
Targets. *See* Victims
Theft, 16, 17, 54

Unemployment, 132
"Urban nomads," 38–39

Urban poor: victimization of, 139
Urban residents: fear of crime, 7, 72

Victims: appearance and, 36–37,
135; approaches to, 97–103;
communication with, 103–5,
136; lethal violence toward, 7,
114, 128, 136; nonlethal violence
toward, 113–15, 116–17, 128,
136; reducing vulnerability of,
134–136; in robber's getaway,
115–18; threat of death and, 96,
103, 104, 107, 116, 128; transfer
of goods (property), 107–15
Victims, criminal, 9–10, 41–42;
targeting of, 62–71, 93–94
Victims, noncriminal: blacks as, 82,
85; injuries to, 7; targeting of,
72–73, 81–88, 94; whites as, 7,
59, 82, 84–85, 94
Violence: in criminal motivation,
57; lethal, 7, 114, 128, 136; nonlethal, 7, 9–10, 87, 113–15,
116–17, 128, 136; threat of, 96,
103, 104, 107, 116, 128

Waters, John, 19
Welfare recipients: victimization of,
139
Whites: as armed robbers, 11; as
criminal victims, 70; as noncriminal victims, 7, 59, 82, 84–85, 94;
targeting of, 64
Wilson, William Julius, 132
Women: as accomplices, 68, 99, 101,
102, 111; as armed robbers,
11–12, 68, 69–70, 99–100; asso-
ciations with armed robbers, 8;
as noncriminal victims, 85–86
Work: attitudes toward, 45–49;
crime prevention and, 131–32